Publications on the Near East

SHIRAZ IN THE AGE OF HAFEZ

THE GLORY OF A MEDIEVAL PERSIAN CITY

JOHN LIMBERT

UNIVERSITY OF WASHINGTON PRESS

Seattle and London

This publication was supported
in part by the Donald R. Ellegood
International Publications Endowment.

Copyright © 2004 by the University of Washington Press
Printed in the United States of America

Library of Congress Cataloging-in-Publication Data
Limbert, John W.
    Shiraz in the age of Hafez : the glory of a medieval Persian city / John Limbert.
        p.   cm.—(Publications on the Near East)
    Includes bibliographical references (p.) and index.
    ISBN 0-295-98391-4 (alk. paper)
    1. Shåråz (Iran)—History.   2. Shåråz (Iran)—Intellectual life.   3. Shåråz
(Iran)—Social life and customs.   4. Shåråz (Iran)—Description and travel.
I. Title.
DS325.S52L56   2004
955'72—dc22
                                                                    2003064510

The paper used in this publication is acid-free and recycled from 10 percent
post-consumer and at least 50 percent pre-consumer waste. It meets the minimum
requirements of American National Standard for Information Sciences—
Permanence of Paper for Printed Library Materials, ANSI z39.48-1984.

Dedicated to the memory of Terence O'Donnell, 1924–2001.
Terry first welcomed us to his Garden of the Brave in War in Shiraz
and helped me open my eyes to what lay hidden in that city.

CONTENTS

PREFACE
AND ACKNOWLEDGMENTS

Throughout history, foreign visitors to Shiraz have praised the city's gardens, its site, its clear air, its wines, and the charm of its people. Today a wine lover will find the city's name memorialized in a delicious red produced (alas) in Australia. Iranians themselves, however, have long treasured Shiraz as a city of Islam. Its traditional Iranian names—*Dar al-Elm* (Abode of Knowledge) and *Borj al-Owlia* (Tower of Saints)—speak to us more of piety and learning than of roses, wine, nightingales, and poetry.

In the fourteenth century C.E. violence and murderous anarchy prevailed in the streets of Shiraz. Through sieges, changes of rule, mob violence, and dynastic strife, the city also provided the setting for a remarkable flourishing of the arts and scholarship. In those years one of its sons, Shams al-Din Mohammad Hafez Shirazi, composed a collection of lyric poetry never equaled before or since. According to the traditional biographies, Hafez spent most of his life in his beloved Shiraz. His verses, even with their infrequent references to famous places and persons, still wove themselves into the spirit and society of his city. His poems remained part of the rich urban life of fourteenth-century Shiraz—both in its body of walls, gates, palaces, shrines, mosques, seminaries, and bazaars, and in its soul of violence, learning, arts, prayers, fasts, and hedonism.

This work looks at the backdrop to Hafez's verses and at the amazing, varied life of fourteenth-century Shiraz where poets composed, scholars studied, mystics sought hidden truths, ascetics prayed and fasted, drunkards brawled, and princes and their courtiers played deadly games of power. This work recounts the history of Shiraz from its founding in the first century of Islam (seventh century C.E.) to its conquest by Amir Timur (Tamerlane) at the end of the fourteenth century. It reconstructs the city's geography and social organization in the age of Hafez. The data for this reconstruction I collected during a four-year residence in Shiraz, where I searched the alleys of the old city for medieval tombstones in forgotten cemeteries and shrines, and spoke to Shirazis who remembered the city in the days before the rebuilding of the Pahlavi era (1925–79) drove new streets through the old quarters.

In recreating the society of the period I used three kinds of prose works: histories of the period; biographies of holy men and women who lived in Shiraz; and accounts of travelers and geographers. Another source is poetry, including both verses from Hafez and those of less well-known Shirazi poets. Although classical Persian poetry rarely describes historical events or social conditions, it remains an inseparable part of the Iranian spirit. Persian poetry is not history, but it does reflect Iranians' intellectual and emotional response to events—a response that Americans might express today in Internet chat rooms, letters to the editor, cartoons, and folk songs.

AN OBLIGATORY NOTE ON NAMES AND DATES

In this history I have kept the cast of characters as clear as possible, although the history of the times sometimes resembles a crowded Russian novel. Here is a brief guide to Muslim names, using as an example the names and titles of the famous Sheikh Ruzbehan of Shiraz (d. 1209):

Title (Laqab)	Nickname (Koniyeh)	Name (Esm)	Patronymic (Nasab)	Family Name (Nesbat)
Sheikh	Abu Mohammad	Ruzbehan	Ali Nasr	Baqli Fasa'i-Shirazi

The Name

The basis and literal center of everyone's name was the given name, or *esm*. In this period, most Iranian Muslims had Arabic names, such as Ali, Osman, and Mohammad, and some had Persian names, such as Bahram, Ruzbeh, or Salbeh. Turkish names such as Abesh and Bozghash also appear, especially among military commanders and the women of the ruling families. This holy man's given name was the Persian Ruzbehan, literally "one whose days are fortunate."

The Nickname

Immediately preceding the *esm* was the *koniyeh* or nickname, such as Abu Mohammad or Abu al-Abbas. The nickname was typically Abu (father of) plus the name of one's eldest son. Sheikh Ruzbehan's nickname was Abu Mohammad. The *koniyeh* was the name most commonly used among friends.

The Title

Before the name and nickname were titles *(laqab),* some purely honorific and others denoting the holder's position in society. Purely honorific titles such as Sadr al-Din, Mo'in al-Din, and Zein al-Din began to appear among high-ranking Shirazis in the late tenth and early eleventh century C.E. Before them came such titles as Qazi (judge), Mowlana (teacher), Sheikh (sufi master), Kalu (bazaar or neighborhood chief), and Khwajeh (nobleman). For example, the sources almost always refer to the chief judge of Fars in Hafez's time as Qazi Majd al-Din—i.e. by his titles. To these titles might be added others like Seyyed (descendent of the prophet) or Amir (originally a military commander, but often simply denoting respect). Ruzbehan's title was simply Sheikh, and in today's Shiraz the neighborhood of his tomb is still called Dar-e-Sheikh.

The Patronymic

Following the name were the patronymics or *nasab* showing the names of ancestors. Although the most common usage was to use the Arabic *ibn* (son of) with the father's name (e.g. Ali b. Hasan for Ali, son of Hasan), the *ibn* might be omitted (e.g. Ali Hasan for Ali b. Hasan). Sometimes a famous but distant ancestor would replace the father's name. For example, Omar b. Yusef b. Salbeh was Omar, son of Yusef, descendent of Salbeh. Ruzbehan's patronymic was Ali Nasr.

The Family Name

Following the given name and patronymic came the *nesbat,* roughly equivalent to the family name. These names (one person often used several of them) indicated a relationship between the individual and a town, a region, an occupation, a tribe, or a famous person (*nesbat* means "relationship"). Among the most common family names in Shiraz during the fourteenth century were Fali, Dashtaki, Hoseini, Alavi, Kuhgiluye'i, and Baghnovi. Ruzbehan had two family names, including Baqli (grocer), and Fasa'i-Shirazi (from Fasa, a small town near Shiraz).

Title of Rank

Further titles, denoting high social position and occupation, were often attached to the family name. These last included such titles as Vazir (minister) and Naqib (leader of the seyyeds).

In any work concerned with Islam and Islamic history, a problem with dates arises from the fact that the lunar Islamic year is eleven days shorter than the solar Gregorian or Zoroastrian years. An Islamic century is therefore about three years shorter than a Christian one. In this work I have used the Christian year which most closely coincides with the Islamic one in the sources.

The transcription system in this work follows modern Persian pronunciation, and there is no attempt to differentiate between the various representations of the sounds *z, s,* and *t*. Specialists will know the original spellings. I have used common English usage where it deviates from this system. For example, Islam, not Eslam; Iraq, not Eraq, except in compounds such as Sheikh al-Eslam, Darvazeh-ye-Esfahan, and Eraq-e-Ajam. Occasionally, there will be diacritical marks added if necessary to avoid confusion.

With acknowledgments I hardly know where to begin. First, I am forever grateful to the people of the old districts of Shiraz, who provided invaluable aid in finding the monuments there. Then to the late Dr. Arthur Upham Pope, by whose kindness I was first able to go to Shiraz and begin research under the auspices of the Asia Institute of Pahlavi University; to Mr. Naser Kojuri of the Fars Office of Arts and Culture; to Mr. Ja'far Vajad, who helped me decipher the fifteenth-century tax inscription discussed in Chapter 4; to Mr. Karamat Ra'na-Hoseini, who introduced the precious source *Shadd al-Izar* to me; to Mr. Paul Enseki of the Asia Institute and Mr. Griff Nelson of the English Department of Pahlavi University, both of whom patiently took many photographs for me; to Dr. Hasan Khub-Nazar, director of the Asia Institute, who generously allowed the use of the Institute's facilities for study and research; to Mrs. Zhaleh Mahluji of the Institute's library; to Mr. N. H. Pirnia of the Office of Preservation of National Monuments in Teheran, who helped me read the inscriptions in Chapter 1; and to many of my students at Pahlavi University, who shared their knowledge of Shirazi tradition.

Special appreciation also goes to Dr. Richard N. Frye of Harvard University, who provided constant guidance, advice, and encouragement for the writing of the dissertation on which this book is based. To Dr. Richard Bulliet, of Columbia University, who suggested much of the methodology, and who offered patient and careful criticism, especially of the details of the second part; to Dr. Beatrice Forbes Manz of Tufts University; and to Mr. Mas'ud Farzad of Pahlavi University in Shiraz, whose vast knowledge of Hafez was especially helpful. Finally, I must acknowledge the assistance of my wife, who provided me with the inspiration and encouragement to complete the work.

The faults in this work are mine, and of course I make no claim to understanding on the basis of having lived in Shiraz. As the poet Sa'adi says,

خر عیسی گرش بمکه برند   چون بیاید هنوز خر باشد

"If they take Jesus' ass to Mecca, When it returns, it is still an ass."

PART ONE

History of Shiraz from Its Founding to the Conquest of Timur

1

History of Shiraz to the Mongol Conquest

روی گفتم که در جهان بنهم
گردم از قید بنگی آزاد

که نه بیرون پارس منزل هست
شام و روم و بصره و بغداد

I said, turn your path to the greater world,
So I should be free of the chains of slavery.

But I found no place for me outside of Fars,
Not Syria, not Anatolia, not Basra, and not Baghdad.

—*Hafez*

ORIGINS

Shiraz is the capital of the Iranian province of Fars, the ancient homeland of the Achemenian (ca. 549–330 B.C.E.) and the Sassanian (ca. 224–651 C.E.) dynasties. The Greeks called this area Persis, from which came our name "Persia" for the entire country. The Iranians derive the name of their beloved national language, Farsi, from the name of this province.

Fars is unique among Iranian provinces in its geography. It consists of a series of plains or valleys *(jolgeh, dasht)* at varying elevations separated from each other by mountain ranges. Each plain, depending on its latitude and elevation, has a distinct climate, and these climates have determined three distinct types of agriculture. The high elevations, or *sardsir,* produce grain, apples, walnuts, mulberries, etc.; the lowlands, or *garmsir* (collective, *garmsirat*), produce dates and citrus; and the temperate or *mo'-tadel* regions produce grain, pomegranates, grapes, and sour oranges.[1] The most famous pre-Islamic Iranian dynasties originated and built their great monuments in these plains—the Achemenians first in the Dasht-e-Mash-had-e-Morghab in the highlands northeast of Shiraz and later in the more temperate plain at Marvdasht; the Sassanians in the subtropical valleys of Darab, Firuzabad, and Kazeron.

Shiraz today sits about 5,500 feet above sea level, in an area of mild climate at the northwestern end of one of those long, narrow plains, which runs northwest to southeast. It has occupied the same site for 1,300 years. The medieval city, although much changed by reconstruction and Pahlavi-era town planning, is located in the eastern and southern parts of the modern town.

Shiraz was not always the capital of Fars, and by Iranian standards it is a new town. Muslim historians agree that the Omayyad Caliph Abd al-Malek b. Marwan founded it in the first/seventh century. A local historian tells us, "It has never been defiled by idol-worship."[2] Another historian, Hamdullah Mostowfi of Qazvin, relates several accounts of the city's origin and concludes:

> The most reliable account, however, is that after the preaching of Islam, Shiraz was founded, or restored, by Mohammad, brother of Hajjaj b. Yusef Thaqafi [Omayyad governor of Iraq]—another version giving it as restored by his cousin Muhammad b. Qasem b. Abi Aqil—the date of its restoration being 74/693.[3]

Pre-Islamic settlement must have existed at or near Shiraz, if only to give the new city its name—notice Mostowfi's use of the word "restored." The anonymous geographer of the *Hodud al-Alam* (tenth century C.E.) reports the existence in Shiraz of two venerated fire temples and an ancient fortress, called Shahmobad.[4] Pre-Islamic remains on the Shiraz plain also indicate the existence of settlement near the site of the present city. There are Sassanian reliefs both east and northwest of Shiraz at Barm-e-Delak and Guyom, respectively, and remains of Sassanian castles at Qasr-e-Abu

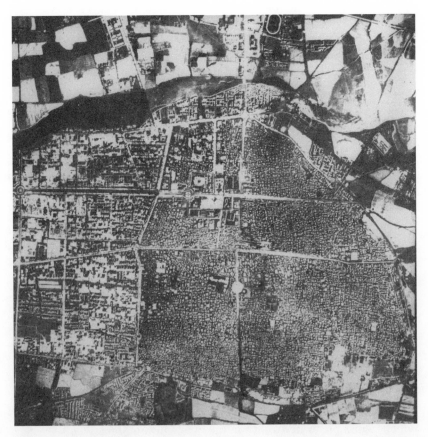

AERIAL VIEW OF SHIRAZ

Nasr, east of the city, and at Qal'eh-ye-Bandar (Fahandezh) near the present Sa'adi village. The latter has been tentatively identified as the geographer's Shahmobad fortress.[5]

Elamite clay tablets from Persepolis contain the name of the castle of Tirazzish, in one version in the form Shirrazish. On late Sassanian and early Islamic clay sealings found at Qasr-e-Abu Nasr appears the name Shiraz, along with Ardashir Khurreh, the Sassanian administrative unit with its capital at Firuzabad, of which this pre-Islamic Shiraz was a part. This evidence suggests that the name Shiraz originated from the Tirrazish (or Shirrazish) of the Elamite tablets and that the name originally applied to a fortress on the site of Qasr-e-Abu Nasr. This settlement, which flourished in the sixth, seventh, and eighth centuries C.E., must have been the center of government for the Shiraz plain until the founding of the present-day city, to which it gave its name.

During the years 640–53, Muslim armies, in a series of expeditions from Basra in southern Iraq, conquered the Sassanian province of Fars, which in its five districts included present-day Fars, Yazd, the Persian Gulf coast and islands, and parts of Khuzestan.[6] The Muslims reached the Shiraz area in 641. There was no city in that region, but there were castles, which agreed to pay tribute to the conquerors. The Sassanian capital of Fars, Estakhr, did not finally submit to Arab rule until 653 following a bloody revolt. During the fighting at Estakhr, the Arabs reportedly used the plain of Shiraz as a camping ground for their army.

SHIRAZ UNDER THE ARAB CALIPHS

The chief town of Fars, Estakhr, had close connections with the Sassanian dynasty and the Zoroastrian faith, and the new Arab rulers wanted to create a rival, Islamic center in their newly conquered territory. When the Arabs originally founded Shiraz, it was laid out to be greater than Esfahan, and to be a thousand paces larger. Despite this auspicious beginning, Shiraz remained a provincial backwater for the first two centuries of its history, overshadowed by its older rival, Estakhr. Estakhr would keep its importance as long as there was a substantial Zoroastrian community in Fars, which would prefer not to live in the new, Muslim Shiraz.

The historian Richard Frye believes that the final decay of Estakhr and the growth of Shiraz coincided with the decay of Zoroastrianism and large-scale conversion to Islam in Fars.[7] The sources say little of this early period, and the city did not have a *jame'* (congregational) mosque until the late ninth century, when the Saffarid rulers established Shiraz as the capital of their semi-independent state.

During this earliest, obscure period of Shiraz's history, important events were shaping the city's future appearance, geography, and social and religious life. By tradition, during the rule of the Abbasid Caliph Ma'-mun (813–833), Abbasid authorities in Shiraz executed several descendents of the Caliph Ali. The martyrs' tombs—often rediscovered after centuries of oblivion—were to become major centers of Shirazi pilgrimage, burial, scholarship, and charity. According to later (Sunni) tradition, in the disturbances following the accession of the Caliph Ma'mun in 813 and the death of the eighth Imam of the Shia, Reza b. Musa Kazem, in 817, three of the Imam's sixteen brothers took refuge in separate houses in Shiraz. According to varying reports, there they either lived in obscurity and died natural deaths, or were executed by the Abbasid governor of Fars.

Shiraz's original group of patron saints was complete when the nephew of these three brothers, Ali b. Hamzeh b. Musa Kazem, fled to Shiraz around 835. There he took refuge in a cave with a few friends and made his living gathering and selling firewood. After a short time Abbasid agents discovered and executed him.

Four centuries passed before thirteenth-century Salghurid rulers and their ministers discovered most of these lost or forgotten graves and endowed them with appropriate monuments. If the original graves do, in fact, antedate the building of the first congregational mosque in Shiraz (894), then their locations, and the sites of other identified early graves, provide an outline of some important points in or near the ancient city. These points were to become centers of the city's religious and economic life.

The location and identification of these graves comes from tradition rather than solid historical evidence, but these traditions are almost the only surviving guide to the earliest period of the city's history. Ali b. Hamzeh's grave was never lost, but over a century passed before Fana Khosrow Azod al-Dowleh, the Shia Deilamite ruler of Shiraz between 950 and 983, restored the grave and improved the site. In the case of Sibawayh the Grammarian (d. 796), the sources are nearly unanimous in locating his grave in the Bahaliyeh district of Shiraz.

The rediscovery of the reputed graves of the three brothers of the eighth Imam, however, had to wait more than four hundred years. According to local tradition, the Amir Moqarreb al-Din Mas'ud, the famous minister of the Salghurid Atabek Abu Bakr b. Sa'd (1226–60), found the grave of Ahmad b. Musa (now famous as Shah-e-Cheragh) while having land cleared for a building near the old congregational mosque. The authorities identified the saint by a seal ring on his miraculously intact body. In the same period, after people saw light emanating from a hill, came discovery of the site presently called Astaneh, the purported grave of Ahmad's brother Hosein. The owner of the property, Atabek Abu Bakr, had the hill excavated and discovered an intact body with a Qoran in one hand and a sword in the other. When the body had been identified (by its "splendor"), the ruler ordered a dome built on the site.[8]

AERIAL VIEW OF THE JAME' ATIQ AREA

Shiraz acquired its congregational mosque in 894, when Amru Leith the Saffarid ordered the construction of the Masjed-Jame (now known as the Jame Atiq, or Old Congregational Mosque). He chose a central location near the bazaar of Shiraz, and later historians report that the Bazar-e-Bozorg (Grand Bazaar) ran to the door of this mosque.[9]

SHIRAZ UNDER THE BUYIDS

Under Buyid rule in the tenth century C.E., Shiraz grew into a large and prosperous town. It was both the capital and largest city of Fars province (including Yazd), followed in importance by Fasa and the port of Siraf. It was a league in circumference and remained without a wall until 1044. Economically, it was of considerable importance, and then, as now, consumed the products of its province rather than raising produce for export. Among the products of Fars noted in the tenth century C.E. were grapes, textiles of linen, wool, and cotton, collyrium, rose water, violet water, palm-blossom water, carpets, and the woven rugs called *zilu* and *gelim*.

The city itself had twelve quarters (called *tassuj*) and eight gates.[10] In 974 Fana Khosrow Azod al-Dowleh Deilami, the greatest ruler of this dynasty, built a suburb for his court and his army south of the city. He named it *Fana Khosrow Gerd* (*gerd* = town or fortress) after himself, and during his reign it became so prosperous that its taxes amounted to 20,000 dinars. But a few years after Azod al-Dowleh's death the Buyids abandoned his city and its palaces, and looted its materials to build fortifications. By the beginning of the twelfth century, as part of the general decline and insecurity, the site had reverted to farms, with a tax value of only 250 dinars.

More substantial Buyid remains still exist in and near Shiraz. There is the original shrine of Ali b. Hamzeh, located just north of the Esfahan Gate. Farther away are the Gonbad-e-Azodiyeh (Azod al-Din's Tower) on the mountains north of the city, and the Band-e-Amir, a dam on the Kur River twenty-five miles to the northeast. Also surviving is Ab-e-Rokni, an underground channel (*qanat*) named after Rokn al-Dowleh Hasan b. Buyeh, the father of Azod al-Dowleh. This channel supplies water to Shiraz from a source nine miles northeast. Long vanished are the Azodiyeh Library and Azodiyeh Hospital (*Dar al-Shafa*), although the name of the latter has survived as a quarter of the old city.

There are also inscriptions, believed to date from Buyid times, located around the city. The most interesting one (p. 10) is the gravestone of Ahmad b. Ali Bishapuri (or Nishapuri). Originally buried near Ali b. Hamzeh, his gravestone was moved to the garden of Haft-tan on the northern edge of the city during rebuilding of the shrine about 1950. Mr. N. H. Pirnia, who helped me read the inscription, believes that this

BUYID (SHIA) INSCRIPTION

Ahmad b. Ali had a Zoroastrian ancestor named Shadhfari, and that he was a Shia, because of the final inscribed "Ali" and the following decorative doubled *vav*, representing Shia twelve in *abjad* numerology.[11] Other surviving Buyid inscriptions are an inscribed *mehrab* (prayer niche) in the hills north of Shiraz, the grave of Abi Zare' Ardebili, and the grave of Sheikh Abu Sa'eb Shami (d. 957), who was famous for owning a hair of the prophet. His grave was popularly called Mu-ye-Rasul (the prophet's hair) or Asar-e-Rasul (the prophet's relic).[12]

Members of the Buyid family were followers of "twelver" Shi'ism, and as such actively encouraged the preaching of this religion by instituting public mourning during Moharram, celebrations of Eid-e-Ghadir, and cursing the enemies of the family of the prophet. But the Buyids, and Azod al-Dowleh in particular, were generally tolerant rulers. They paid the greatest respect to the famous Sunni saint and mystic of Shiraz, Abdullah b. Khafif Sheikh-e-Kabir (882–982). Azod al-Dowleh's son, Sharaf al-Dowleh Shirzil (r.983–89) built a *khaneqah* (dervish lodge) for the sheikh's followers outside the city gates.

In Buyid times, Fars was famous for having the largest Zoroastrian population of any Moslem province—every region possessed a fire temple. The non-Moslems of Shiraz wore no special mark to distinguish themselves, and the bazaars of the town were illuminated during Iranian festivals such as Mehregan and Nowruz. In 369/980, when the Moslems of Shiraz rioted against the Zoroastrians, Azod al-Dowleh sent troops to punish the rioters.

THE SELJUQS AND SALGHURIDS IN FARS
The successors of Azod al-Dowleh were unable to maintain the same level of security and prosperity. Buyid family squabbles, Turkmen incursions, and religious-tribal uprisings in Fars forced the last strong Buyid ruler, Abu Kalijar Marzuban, to build the first wall around the city in 1048. In 1062 Fazluyeh, the leader of the Shabankareh federation, a group of tribes centered on Darabgerd and Ij, drove the next Buyid ruler, Fulad-Sotun, out of Fars. In the same year Seljuq Turkish forces defeated Fazluyeh, and the *khotbeh* (Friday sermon) in Shiraz was read in Sultan Toghril Beg's name. Fazluyeh submitted to the Seljuqs, and remained as tributary ruler of Shiraz. But five years later Fars was in revolt again and the Seljuqs finally defeated and killed Fazluyeh in 1068.[13]

Troubles with the Shabankareh, however, did not end with the death of their leader. Throughout the second half of the fifth/eleventh century, Shabankareh uprisings, which the Seljuq governor of Fars could not control, tore the province apart and nearly destroyed Shiraz. Firuzabad, numerous castles in Fars, and the entire district of Shapur Khurreh (the Kazeroun and Bishapur region) defied Seljuq authority. The eleventh-century *Farsnameh* of Ibn Balkhi describes this anarchic period as follows:

> When, at the end of Deilamite rule, struggles occurred between Fazluyeh and Qavurt, Shiraz and its region were successively looted and ruined. Shiraz was looted twice a year, by the Shabankareh from one direction and by the Turks and Turkmen from the other. They took and confiscated whatever they found until the people were left destitute. The hope is that now [1108] matters will return to normal.[14]

Shiraz did not recover her peace and stability until the second Seljuq Atabek, Chaveli (r.1099–1117), had pacified the Shabankareh, rebuilt the city walls, and destroyed the many castles which had become centers of rebellion in Fars.

This episode of the Shabankareh illustrates a recurring theme in the history of Shiraz: the city's precarious and transient prosperity. The well-being of Shiraz has always depended on the security of its surrounding region, and that security has always been delicate. Fars has always been a land of simmering anarchy, where the sparse settled population, isolated towns, and difficult communication have fostered insecurity and the growth of independent tribal confederations. Although Fars is naturally productive and prosperous, even today the prosperity of Shiraz is fragile, depending on a strong authority to preserve security in the hinterland.

The fortunes of Shiraz improved when, in 1148, Songhor b. Mowdud drove out the Seljuq ruler of Fars. Songhor, who had served with a previous Atabek (regent) of Shiraz, Bozabeh (r.1140–46), founded the dynasty of the Salghurid Atabeks, who ruled Shiraz for 120 years as nominal vassals of the Seljuqs, the Khwarezmshahs, and the Mongols. Although Salghurid times were far from peaceful, during that era Shiraz regained her prosperity, received many new buildings, and became a leading center of Islamic scholarship. Most important, the Salghurids, thanks to timely submission, diplomacy, and bribery, shielded Shiraz from the ravages of Khwarezmshah and Mongol invaders.

Despite the Salghurids' best efforts, however, during this period Fars was under constant assault by members of the Seljuq family, by the Khwarezmshahs, and (again) by Shabankareh. These last had profited from prevailing confusion to rebuild the castles Amir Chaveli had destroyed. From neighboring Kerman, the Shabankareh would raid into Fars, then withdraw into their impregnable fortresses when faced with a Salghurid army.

The fourth Salghurid ruler, Sa'd b. Zangi (r. 1194–1226), had to fight a devastating, eight-year civil war with his cousin to gain undisputed possession of the throne. Sa'd momentarily pacified the Shabankareh, rebuilt the walls of Shiraz, and added Kerman to the Salghurid realm. Sa'd later became tributary to Ala al-Din Mohammad Khwarezmshah after the latter defeated him in 1217.

The historians credit the next ruler of the dynasty, Atabek Abu Bakr b. Sa'd (r. 1226–60) with solving two hitherto unsolvable problems: the final pacification of the Shabankareh, and the successful defense of Fars against the invasions of Ghiyath al-Din, the brother of Sultan Jalal al-Din Khwarezmshah. But nothing does Abu Bakr, and in fact all of the Salghurids, so much credit as his policy of timely submission to superior forces, particularly those of the Mongols. The historian Vassaf describes the Atabek's statesmanship as follows:

> He submitted to and sent his nephew to Ogedai Qa'an [the son of Changhiz Khan] and paid tribute. Ogedai received him favorably, gave Abu Bakr the title Qotlogh Khan, and did not disturb his territory. Thus Shiraz remained safe from all the horror of the times . . . Every year he sent the [Mongol] Khan 30,000 dinars as tribute, adding pearls and other valuables. Every year he would send his son Atabek Sa'd or one of his nephews to the Khan. He settled the Mongol officials outside the town and supplied them there, forbidding the ordinary people from going there, lest the Mongols realize the state of the country.[15]

This was the Salghurids' greatest achievement: during the thirteenth century they kept Shiraz safe from the ravages of the Mongols, who were perpetrating slaughter and destruction in northern Iran. The Salghurid rulers also endowed the city with fine buildings, some of which still stand. The first ruler of the line, Songhor b. Mowdud (r. 1148–61) built a complex of buildings in the Bagh-e-Now district, including the Songhoriyeh Seminary and Mosque, which two hundred years later, according to the sources, were still among the finest public buildings in the city. All trace of them has now vanished.

Songhor's brother, Zangi b. Mowdud (r. 1161–75), built a *rabat* (dervish center) at the tomb of Sheikh-e-Kabir, who had died two centuries earlier and whose grave had fallen into obscurity.[16] The next ruler, Atabek Sa'd b. Zangi, founded what is still the largest (but ruined) building in Shiraz, the Masjed-e-Now (New Mosque), about a quarter mile west of the Old Congregational Mosque. Sa'd's son Abu Bakr, had a dome built over the site of the newly discovered grave of Seyyed Amir Ahmad b. Musa (today's famous Shah-e-Cheragh), almost midway between the old and new mosques. Southeast of the city, Abu Bakr's granddaughter, Abesh bint Sa'd (630–688/1233–87), built the famous Rabat-e-Abesh near the grave of her ancestors. This building still stood in 1972 under the names Abesh Khatun and Khatun-e-Qiyamat, and nearby is an inscription (opposite page) from the grave of a Salghurid princess who died in 661/1263.[17]

In religious matters, the liberal spirit of the Buyid age yielded to a more rigid orthodoxy under the Salghurids. Atabek Abu Bakr was so strict on religious matters that under his rule "no one had the courage to study logic or philosophy."[18] He expelled philosophy teachers and all scholars propagating unorthodox ideas. When the Atabek heard that one of the leading Alavis of Shiraz, Amir Asil al-Din Abdullah, had decided to leave the city because of the prevalence of "unbelief" there, the ruler forbade *ma'arakeh* (religious shows with Shia overtones) and ordered the people to read only Sunni books.[19]

These centuries of Turkish rule in Shiraz also featured prominent ministers of Iranian origin, usually members of patrician families of Fars, who rivaled their masters in endowing public works. Under the Seljuq Atabek Bozabeh and his successors, for example, the minister Taj al-Din Abu'l-Fath b. Darast Shirazi (in office ca. 1130–50) endowed a seminary named after himself (the Madraseh-ye-Taji). The name Banjir of Taj al-Din's deputy, Amin al-Din Abu Hasan Banjir Kazeruni, suggests a Deilamite origin. Amin al-Din later served as minister of the Salghurid ruler Tekleh

INSCRIPTION FROM THE GRAVE OF A SALGHURID PRINCESS (D. 1263)

b. Zangi (r. 1175–94) and endowed the Madraseh-ye-Amini next to the Old Congregational Mosque.

The Minister of Atabek Sa'd b. Zangi (1194–1226), Khwajeh Amid al-Din Abu Nasr As'ad Farsi Afzari (Fazari), came from one of the most noble families of Fars. The family of Afzari, named for a district in the lowlands, was famous for supplying the qazi al-qozat (chief judge) of Fars since the reign of Azod al-Dowleh in the tenth century. Amid al-Din himself is most famous for composing the poem "Qasideh-ye-Amid" or "Qasideh-ye-Ashknavan" while imprisoned (in the Ashknavan fortress) and awaiting execution at the hands of Atabek Sa'd's son, Abu Bakr, in 1226.[20]

Moqarreb al-Din Mas'ud b. Badr (d. 1258) was minister of Atabek Abu Bakr b. Sa'd (1226–1260). This very wealthy minister was famous for his discovery of the grave of Ahmad b. Musa and for his generous endowments of pious foundations, including the eponymous seminary, Madraseh-ye-Moqarrebi, in the main bazaar near the Old Congregational Mosque. Fifty years after his death, his endowments, despite encroachments and corruption, still totaled thirty thousand dinars a year.

Unlike other ministers of this period, Fakhr al-Din Abu Bakr b. Abu Nasr Havayeji was of lowly origin–his father, as his *nesbat* "Havayeji" shows, was a supplier, or forager, for the royal kitchen. He served as minister of Atabek Abu Bakr until that ruler's death in 1260. Afterwards, Torkan Khatun, the new Atabek's mother and regent, had him secretly executed during the reign of Mohammad b. Sa'd b. Abu Bakr (r. 1260–62). Among the institutions he founded were a mosque and seminary in the Atabek's palace compound.

CONCLUSION: FROM BACKWATER TO METROPOLIS

During the first centuries of its life, Shiraz grew from a provincial backwater, overshadowed by its famous neighbor Estakhr, into a prosperous center of learning and pilgrimage under Buyid patronage. But this prosperity always remained fragile, requiring the ruler to maintain both internal stability and control over unruly surrounding tribes. When both of these broke down for almost a century under the last Buyids and the Seljuq Atabeks, Shiraz went into serious decline.

The long, stormy reign of the Salghurids, beginning in the middle of the twelfth century, saw Shiraz regain its cultural preeminence, when Turkish rulers and their Iranian ministers provided both security and patronage for buildings, the arts, and scholarship. Those conditions allowed individual geniuses such as the mystic Sheikh Ruzbehan (1128–1209) and the poet Sa'di (d. 1293), and families of scholars such as the Baghnovi, Fali-Sirafi, Alavi, Salmani, and Adib-Salehani (see Chapter 6 and appendix), to turn Shiraz into a flourishing center of Islamic culture. The same rulers and ministers endowed the city with buildings worthy of a seat of government and learning, and the wise Salghurid policy of submission to greater Turkish or Mongol force kept the city physically and socially intact despite the ever-present insecurity of the era.

2

Things Fall Apart:
Shiraz under the Mongols
and Their Successors

نگفتمت که به ترکان نظر مکن سعدی

O Sa'adi, did I not tell you not to look at the Turks?

—Sa'adi

THE SALGHURIDS SELF-DESTRUCT

Things fell apart in Shiraz soon after the death of Atabek Abu Bakr b. Sa'd in 1260. After the harsh and tough-minded Salghurid rulers, who had known when to yield to superior force, came a series of drunkards, braggarts, and children. Abu Bakr's immediate successor was his son Sa'd, who was returning from attendance at the Mongol camp at the time of his father's death. Before reaching Shiraz, he sickened and died at Tafresh after only twelve days of rule.

Following Sa'd came his young son, Azod al-Din Mohammad b. Sa'd. The young Atabek's mother, Torkan Khatun, brought her husband's body to Shiraz and buried him in the Madraseh-ye-Azodiyeh (named for their son) which she had founded in the Bagh-e-Now district. Then the Khatun, acting as regent, ordered the previous minister secretly executed (see above, Chapter 1) and replaced him with the able Nezam al-Din Abu Bakr. She also took the essential step of sending letters and presents to the Mongol ruler Hulagu Khan, who confirmed her son's right to rule in Fars. Two

Table 2.1. The Last Salghurids

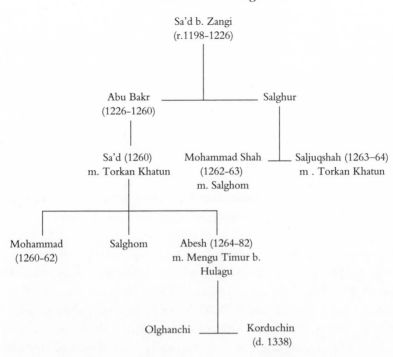

years later, however, the young ruler died after falling off a roof. His mother lamented:

این چه باداست که او غنچهٔ نشکفته بریخت   وین چه سیل است که بر کند ز بن شمشادم

What wind is this that tore off the flower bud?
And what flood is this that uprooted my lofty evergreen?

The next two rulers brought disaster to the Salghurid family. Mohammad Shah b. Salghur b. Sa'd b. Zangi, a nephew of Atabek Abu Bakr (see table 2.1), married Salghom, the daughter of Torkan Khatun. While this ruler spent most of his time in drunken orgies, his brother Saljuqshah, imprisoned in the castle of Estakhr, wrote an appeal for release.

درد و غم و بند من درازی دارد   عیش و طرب تو سر فرازی دارد

بر هر دو مکن تکیه که دوران فلک   در پرده هزار گونه بازی دارد

> My chains are long and my pain and sorrow are deep.
> Your pleasure and music are lofty.
> Rely neither on this depth nor that height,
> For destiny has a thousand tricks up its sleeve.

Mohammad Shah ignored this advice, but after a few months of debauchery, Torkan and her advisers arrested him and delivered him to Hulagu.[1] The Shirazis illuminated the city and Saljuqshah was freed from prison and placed on the throne.

Like his brother, the new ruler lived only for wine and pleasure. He married Torkan (who must have been much older than he), but in a fit of drunkenness had a slave murder her. He then turned on the Mongol officers in Shiraz and killed them and their households. Shams al-Din Miyaq, who had been Torkan's lover and a slave-officer in her first husband's court, escaped to the Mongol camp and reported the state of affairs in Shiraz. Hulagu's response was to execute Mohammad Shah and send an army to Shiraz. Contingents from Lorestan, Shabankareh, and Yazd, where the ruler, Atabek Ala al-Dowleh, hoped to avenge the murder of his sister Torkan, joined the Mongol forces. Saljuqshah foolishly defied the Mongols, ignored offers of clemency, and was defeated and captured at Kazeroun in 1264. Soon afterwards the Mongols murdered him at the Qal'eh-ye-Sefid.[2]

The Shirazis had disliked Torkan Khatun because of her illicit relationship with her husband's officer, Miyaq. They had also considered her "ill-omened" (bad-qadam) because, soon after she married Atabek Abu Bakr's son Sa'd, the Mongols killed the last Abbasid caliph (1258) and ended that five-hundred-year-old dynasty. But despite these poor notices, and despite some Iranian historians' criticisms of the "corrupting influence of the Turkish and Mongol khatuns," Torkan should earn credit for working to save Salghurid rule in Fars with the most unpromising male material.[3]

Shiraz had seen four Atabeks in four years, and now the only surviving members of the Salghurid family were Salghom and Abesh, the daughters of Sa'd b. Abu Bakr. Thus, in 1264, coins were minted and the prayers for the ruler at the Friday sermon were read in the name of Abesh bint Sa'd b. Abu Bakr. She ruled independently, however, for only one year— until 1265, when she married Hulagu's son Mengu Timur. With this union, effective Salghurid rule ended in Fars and the province came under direct Mongol control, which lasted, in one form or another, until the death of the last ruling Il-Khan, Abu Sa'id Bahador, in 1335.

FIGHTING FOR THE SPOILS

Mongol governors, officials, and tax contractors in Shiraz could count on tenures as stable as that of a Dodge City sheriff.[4] Among the many governors who came and went so frequently during this period, two factions waged a brutal struggle for the support of the Il-Khan, the key to power in Fars. One group, centered around Seyyed Emad al-Din Abu Torab, treated Shiraz as occupied territory to be milked for as much revenue as possible as quickly as possible. This group predominated during the governorship of Suqunchaq No'in (in office c. 1271–81), who remained in the Mongol camp in Azarbaijan and left Fars to the mercy of his tax agents *(basqaq)*. By their uncontrolled demands, these agents and tax farmers *(moqate')* in the long run brought greater ruin to the economy of Fars than did any destruction by the Mongol armies. The collectors squeezed the inhabitants not only to enrich themselves, but also to pay for gifts to superiors, for trips to the Mongol camp, and for interest on loans.

A second faction, although no less self-interested or avaricious, took a longer-term view of its own welfare. This party centered around Atabek Abesh Khatun (d. 685/1286) and her allies Khwajeh Nezam al-Din Vazir and Jalal al-Din Arghan, her distant cousin. This party also had support from many influential Shirazis, and, in the case of Abesh herself, from the urban lower classes.[5]

The battle between the two parties intensified when, in 1284, the Il-Khan granted Emad al-Din complete power in Fars and ordered him to send Abesh to the Mongol camp for questioning. When the new governor reached Shiraz he began settling accounts with his enemies and ignoring Abesh. She, in return, ignored his order to report to the Mongol camp. Later that same year the stalemate between the two parties ended when a group of Abesh's partisans assassinated Emad al-Din in the bazaar. When the Shirazis realized what had happened they illuminated the town in celebration.

The victory of the Atabek's party, however, was short-lived. When the Il-Khan learned what had happened to his appointed official in Shiraz, he ordered Abesh and her counselors to attend him at court as soon as possible. Infuriated by their evasive replies and attempts at bribery, he sent officers to Shiraz to investigate Emad al-Din's killing. They arrested the Atabek's counselors, but out of respect for her as a member of a royal family and the daughter-in-law of Hulagu, made no move against Abesh herself until Arghun Khan sent explicit instructions to bring her and her advisors immediately to Tabriz. There he executed Abesh's cousin Jalal al-Din, and ordered the rest of her party to pay a heavy fine to heirs of the murdered Emad al-Din. Abesh, the last of the Salghurids, took sick and died in Tabriz in 1286. Her body was brought to Shiraz and buried in her own *rabat* (shrine complex), which still stands under her name (see chapter 1). Mourning for her death, the historian Vassaf recited this verse:

وارث ملک سلیمان رفت در خاك ای دریغ

کو سلیمان تا بدان بلقیس خوش بگریستی

Alas, the heir of the realm of Solomon has gone to the grave
Where is Solomon, to weep for this fair Sheba?

The Il-Khan kept the late Atabek Abesh's officers, including Nezam al-Din Vazir and Seif al-Din Yusef, at the Mongol camp in Tabriz, where they accumulated enormous debts. To extricate themselves, they agreed, in return for power in Fars, to pay all the back taxes of the province—half a million dinars—to the central treasury. Although there was no possibility of squeezing so much money from that unfortunate province, squeeze they did. When they were unable to deliver the full amount due, the Il-Khan sent Jowshi, one of his most ruthless officers, to finish collecting. Jowshi taxed shade trees, ferreted out misers' hidden hordes, and, in 1290, executed former officials, including both Khwajeh Nezam al-Din and Seif al-Din.

There seems little to choose between there two competing factions. Although the Shirazis themselves had a sentimental attachment to Atabek Abesh, she exercised little authority. Both sides were equally determined to collect as much as possible for themselves, out of greed and out of the need to buy security against the day of their inevitable downfall and accounting. The Atabek's party, thanks to its support from the Shirazi aristocrats, could apply methods of revenue extraction slightly less harsh than those of its opponents, who relied on brute force and the power of the central government to hold their positions.[6] Although some officials would consider the welfare of the city in their actions, the uncertainty of their tenure and the prevailing anarchy in Fars, which was raided by Nikudar Mongols in 1278 and 1300, prevented anyone's establishing stable rule and coherent policies.[7]

The sources report that the two most able rulers of this difficult period were non-Muslims. The first, Enkiyanu, the Mongol governor from 1269 to 1271, received praise from Muslim historians for his foresight and ability. He allowed previous officials to keep their offices, but strictly punished any who disobeyed his orders to observe fair dealing. He enjoyed discussing abstruse questions of Islamic theology with the sheikhs of the town.[8] The other able non-Moslem ruler of Shiraz was Shams al-Dowleh, whom the Shirazis called Malek al-Yahud (King of the Jews). Appointed by the Il-Khan Arghun Khan (r. 1284–1291) and his Jewish minister Sa'd al-Dowleh, he came to Shiraz in 1289 with the infamous Jowshi. Unlike Jowshi, however, he acted fairly and with moderation toward the Shirazis, and kept the Mongol officers from overstepping the bounds of their traditional law (the *yasa*). Shams al-Dowleh cultivated the support of the religious classes and protected Islam in Shiraz; he claimed to be Moslem and said that he remained outwardly Jewish for political purposes. He must have been an exceptionally able governor, for when his patron Sa'd al-Dowleh was killed just before the death of Arghun in 1291, Shiraz escaped the anti-Jewish lootings and massacres that occurred throughout the Il-Khanid empire. Shams al-Dowleh was able to keep his position in Fars for a year after the death of his patron.

Between the death of Atabek Abu Bakr in 1260 and the accession of Shah Sheikh Abu Eshaq Inju in 1343, Shiraz enjoyed a few brief periods of security and stable government. Such periods, however, were merely interludes in the prevailing anarchy. A major cause of this anarchy was the Mongol practice of selling governorships and the insecure tenure of the buyers. To gain his post, an aspirant made rich gifts to influential officials at the Il-Khan's court. After his appointment, the governor could either stay at the camp and entrust direct rule and revenue collection to his agents, or he could go to the province and personally supervise matters. If he resided in his province he would be vulnerable to intrigues of his enemies at the camp, and he might find himself replaced and recalled for accounting and *siyasat* (punishment and torture) for real or imagined misdeeds. But if he stayed at the camp to defend his position, he would have no power over the actions of his agents, who would zealously collect revenue, mostly for themselves, and deliver little of it to the central treasury. When the agents' greed got out of hand (as it always did), stories would reach the court, perhaps through the *shahneh* (police official) of the town, and again the governor would find his position endangered.

These changes of governor and revenue scandals happened repeatedly in Fars. The sources tell of numerous newly appointed governors of Fars whose first assignment was to "straighten out the finances and collect back taxes owed to the government."[9] Thus, in 1281, when the Mongol officer Toghachar accompanied Seyyed Emad al-Din to Shiraz on such a mission, their first act was to arrest their predecessors (including the Seyyed's old enemy, Nezam al-Din Vazir), "investigate" their finances, and extract from them what they owed.

In the midst of this turbulent period, from around 1293 to 1325, the Tibi family controlled much of Fars (see table 2.2). The first member of this family the sources mention is Jamal al-Din Ebrahim, a wealthy merchant of Arab origin who, in 1293, paid Geikhatu Khan (1291–95) ten million dinars for the right to collect taxes from the Inju (crown land) in Fars for four years. There are many stories of Jamal al-Din's fabulous wealth, much of which came from maritime trade with India and China.[10] In return for timely and generous gifts to the Il-Khan, his wives, and the Mongol commanders, Jamal al-Din received the title Malek-e-Eslam and, more important, the right to collect taxes in Fars without interference from Mongol officials.

Although the accounts in the sources are confusing, the Malek-e-Eslam never held independent power for more than a few years at a time. The breakdown of coherent administration under the early Il-Khans flooded the provinces with civil, military, and revenue officials, all pressing conflicting claims to authority. The fortunes of the Malek-e-Eslam in Fars depended on the outcome of his unending struggles with competing revenue collectors.[11]

Jamal al-Din, although constrained by his uncertain tenure, partially

Table 2.2 The Tibi Family

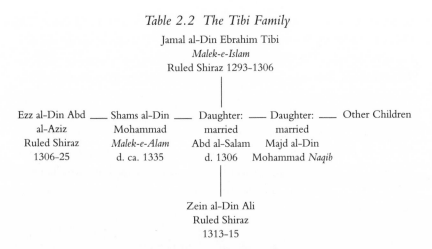

Jamal al-Din Ebrahim Tibi
Malek-e-Islam
Ruled Shiraz 1293–1306

Ezz al-Din Abd —— Shams al-Din —— Daughter: —— Daughter: —— Other Children
al-Aziz   Mohammad   married   married
Ruled Shiraz   *Malek-e-Alam*   Abd al-Salam   Majd al-Din
1306–25   d. ca. 1335   d. 1306   Mohammad *Naqib*

Zein al-Din Ali
Ruled Shiraz
1313–15

shielded the inhabitants of Fars from the greed of Mongol tax collectors by forgiving debts and advancing seed and other supplies to the peasants. He also allied himself to the Shirazi aristocracy by marrying one of his daughters to Seyyed Majd al-Din Mohammad, the Naqib (chief of the seyyeds) of Shiraz. After Jamal al-Din's death in 1306, one of his numerous sons, Ezz al-Din Abd al-Aziz, succeeded him and took the title Malek e-Adel. The Il-Khan Oljaitu (r. 1304–1316) confirmed Ezz al-Din as governor of Shiraz, but, like his father, he had to struggle to keep his position. For the most part he stayed at the Mongol camp and ruled Fars through his agent.

In 1319, the Il-Khan Abu Sa'id Bahador (r. 1316–35) made Korduchin, the daughter of Abesh and Mengu Timur (see above), sole ruler of Fars in gratitude for her deft handling of affairs there after the death of his predecessor, Sultan Oljaitu. Control of Fars shifted between Korduchin and Sheikh Ezz al-Din until 1325, when the latter fell victim to the intrigues of Dameshq Khajeh Chupani at the Mongol court at Sultaniyeh.[12] Ezz al-Din's death marked the end of Tibi power in Fars, although his brother Shams al-Din Mohammad spent ten years at the Mongol court lobbying unsuccessfully for his late brother's post.

THE COMING OF THE INJU

Sharaf al-Din Mahmud, who traced his ancestry to the famous scholar Khwajeh Abdullah Ansari of Herat (1006–1089), was in the service of Amir Chupan Salduz, the great commander of Sultan Abu Sa'id Bahador.[13] While

Korduchin was still nominal ruler in Fars, Amir Chupan sent Sharaf al-Din Mahmud to Shiraz as tax agent to supervise the inju, or the personal hold-ings of the Sultan. Through his ability, Sharaf al-Din soon gained both finan-cial control of southern Iran and a personal fortune with a yearly income of one million dinars. He remained at the Mongol court at Soltaniyeh, where he received the title Shah Mahmud Inju, and put his sons, Jalal al-Din Mas'ud Shah, Ghiyath al-Din Keikhosrow, and Shams al-Din Mohammad, in con-trol of the provinces (see table 2.3). At the court he was a protege of the Il-Khan's minister, Khwajeh Ghiyath al-Din b. Rashid al-Din Fazlullah (son of the great minister and historian), and the two families formed a mar-riage alliance.[14]

Table 2.3. The Inju Family

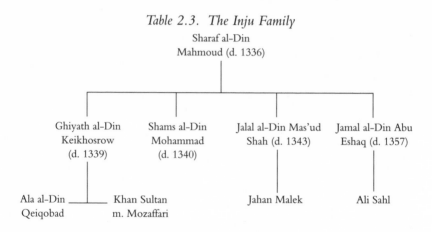

As long as there was a strong central Mongol authority, families like the Inju (and the Tibi before them) depended entirely on the capricious good-will of the Il-Khan. In 1334, the ruler Abu Sa'id (for reasons not mentioned in the sources) removed Shah Mahmud from his position as governor of Fars and replaced him with a Mongol officer, Amir Mosafer Inaq. Mah-mud Shah, however, fearing for his wealth and emboldened by years in power, conspired with his supporters to kill his rival, and pursued him to the walls of Abu Sa'id's palace in Soltaniyeh. When Amir Mosafer took refuge there, the conspirators did not give up, but attacked the very palace of the Il-Khan.

Abu Sa'id was furious at this bold plot, but, at Ghiyath al-Din Rashidi's intervention, refrained from killing the plotters and imprisoned each of them in separate castles. He put Mahmud Shah in the Tabarak castle of

Esfahan, and his oldest son, Jalal al-Din Mas'ud Shah, in Anatolia. The conspirators, except for Mahmud Shah and his son, stayed in prison until Abu Sa'id's death in 1335. Those two were soon freed (again at the intervention of Khwajeh Ghiyath al-Din).[15]

Amir Mosafer Inaq had little opportunity to enjoy his governorship of Fars. The Inju family representative in Shiraz, Ghiyath al-Din Keikhosrow, second son of Shah Mahmud, ignored the new governor and on various pretexts blocked his taking control of the province. When news of Abu Sa'id's death reached Shiraz, Keikhosrow arrested Amir Mosafer and sent him back to the Mongol court at Soltaniyeh.

After the death of Abu Sa'id, the Mongol court was most unhealthy for the courtiers. Both Mahmud Shah and his protector Ghiyath al-Din Rashidi lost their lives in the first months of the bloody ten-year struggle that followed the death of the last Il-Khan. Following the first wave of executions, murders, and vengeance killings, a struggle emerged between Sheikh Hasan-e-Kuchek b. Teimur Tash b. Amir Chupan and Sheikh Hasan-e-Bozorg Ilkani, a descendant of one of Hulagu's commanders.[16]

Sheikh Hasan-e-Bozorg eventually founded the Jalayerid, or Ilkani, dynasty at Baghdad, while his rival, Sheikh Hasan-e-Kuchek Chupani, ruled at Tabriz through Soleiman, a puppet Il-Khan, until 1343. In that year Sheikh Hasan's wife, Ezzat Malek Khatun, fearing for her own and her lover's life, killed her husband by crushing his testicles. The poet Salman of Saveh, who enjoyed the patronage of the Chupanis' rival, Hasan-e-Bozorg, celebrated the death of his patron's enemy as follows:

ز هجرت نبوی رفته هفتصد و چل و چهار   در آخر رجب افتاد اتفاق حسن

زنی چگونه زنی خیر خیرات جهان   بزور بازوی خود خصیتین شیخ حسن

گرفت محکم و میداشت تا بمرد و برفت   زهی خجسته زنی خایه دار مرد افکن

In the year 744 Hijra occurred a blessed event at the end of Rajab.
A woman, such a woman, the best of the world, by the strength
    of her arm
Grasped the testicles of Sheikh Hasan and held them firmly until
    he died.
Well done! Fortunate, courageous, man-conquering woman![17]

But in spite of (or perhaps because of) the poet's praise, her late hus-band's men murdered Ezzat Malek in revenge, carved up the corpse, and devoured the pieces.[18]

While the members of the Il-Khan's court were slaughtering each other, Shiraz was, as always, imitating the fashions of the capital. The years from the death of Abu Sa'id in 1335 to Shah Sheikh Abu Eshaq Inju's taking undisputed control in Fars in 1343 were years of anarchy and a complex, many-sided struggle for power among regional warlords. The major contenders in Shiraz were the four sons of Shah Mahmud Inju, members of the Chupani family, Sheikh Hasan-e-Bozorg, and Mobarez al-Din Mohammad Mozaffar, the ruler of Yazd.

Round One: The Inju Brothers Fight among Themselves

In the confusion following the death of Abu Sa'id, Jalal al-Din Mas'ud Shah b. Mahmud Shah Inju left the Mongol court at Soltaniyeh and returned to Shiraz. His younger brother, Ghiyath al-Din Keikhosrow, who had been ruling there in the name of their father since 1326, refused to surrender power. In 1337 fighting broke out between the two brothers after Amir Keikhosrow killed his brother's minister. Mas'ud Shah was vic-torious, and imprisoned both Keikhosrow and another brother, Shams al-Din Mohammad, in the White Fortress *(Qal'eh-ye-Sefid)*. Keikhosrow died there in 1338, but Mohammad escaped and fled to Esfahan.

Round Two: The Chupanis Enter the Battle

Sheikh Hasan-e-Kuchek, hoping to regain control of the provinces for his so-called "central" government in Tabriz, named his cousin Pir Hosein b. Amir Mahmud b. Amir Chupan governor of Fars (see table 2.4). In 1339 Pir Hosein and Shams al-Din Mohammad Inju joined forces and defeated Mas'ud Shah at Sarvestan. The allies entered Shiraz, and the defeated Mas'ud Shah fled to Lorestan. A month later, Pir Hosein executed Amir Mohammad Inju on a pretext and took sole control of Shiraz. What hap-pened next is unclear. Shirazi historian Zarkub, writing a few years after the events described, says that the enraged Shirazis rose up and drove Pir Hosein and his men out of the city.[19] Ibn Battuta embellishes the episode (although he has confused some of the names and dates) to illustrate the power of chivalry among the Shirazis. He writes:

Table 2.4. The Chupani Family

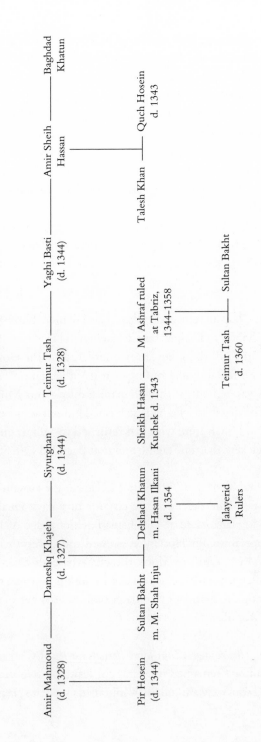

Pir Hosein arrested Tash Khatun [wife of Mahmud Shah] and her
son Abu Eshaq to take them to Tabriz, there to question them about
Mahmud Shah's property. When this group reached the center of
the Shiraz bazaar, Tash Khatun removed her veil. The *khatun,* as is
the custom with Turkish women, usually went out with her face
uncovered; however this time she had covered her face from shame.
She appealed to the Shirazis for help, saying, "O men of Shiraz! I
am the wife of so-and-so, my name is so-and-so. Will you allow
me to be taken this way?" A carpenter named Pahlavan Mahmud
(I saw him in the bazaar) rose and said, "No, we won't allow it. We
won't allow her to be taken from Shiraz!" The people joined him,
a riot ensued, and all the Shirazis took up arms. They killed many
of the soldiers, captured booty, and rescued the *khatun* and her son.
Amir Pir Hosein fled Shiraz. . . .[20]

Pir Hosein Chupani returned to the service of his cousin, Sheikh Hasan-
e-Kuchek, in Tabriz and helped him defeat his rival Hasan-e-Bozorg Ilkani.
In gratitude, in 1340 the Chupani strongman gave Pir Hosein an army
to recapture Shiraz and take revenge on its inhabitants. Joining him in
this venture was a client of the Chupani family, Amir Mobarez al-Din
Mohammad b. Mozaffar, who had established himself as independent ruler
of Yazd. Mas'ud Shah Inju, who had returned to Shiraz, once again fled
before the attackers, this time taking refuge at Baghdad with Sheikh Hasan-
e-Bozorg.[21]

With Mas'ud Shah gone, the Shirazis, fearing Pir Hosein's vengeance,
closed their gates and defended the city for fifty days. Finally the intervention of Mowlana Majd al-Din Esma'il, chief judge of Fars, brought
about a compromise. Pir Hosein reassumed the governorship of Shiraz
peacefully and agreed to overlook the city's past resistance. Pir Hosein
rewarded Mohammad Mozaffar's service by adding Kerman to his domin-
ions, thus laying the foundation for later bloody wars between the houses
of Inju and Mozaffar.[22]

Round Three: The Youngest Inju Joins (Briefly) a Rival Chupani
Pir Hosein himself remained in Shiraz for less than two years, while the
two surviving sons of Mahmud Shah Inju made separate plans for retaking

Fars and avenging the murder of their brother Amir Mohammad. For this purpose Abu Eshaq, the youngest brother, allied himself with Malek Ashraf b. Teimur Tash b. Chupan, a brother of Hasan-e-Kuchek and a cousin of Pir Hosein. Abu Eshaq had been ruling in Esfahan, where Pir Hosein had placed him to counter the growing influence of his "ally" in Yazd and Kerman, Mohammad Mozaffar. In 1342 Malek Ashraf and Abu Eshaq joined forces at Esfahan, and, when Pir Hosein heard of their plans, he moved to attack them there. Pir Hosein was defeated, and, mistrusting Mohammad Mozaffar, returned to Tabriz, where Hasan-e-Kuchek had him eliminated.

Round Four: More Injus and More Chupanis Arrive

The victorious allies, Abu Eshaq and Malek Ashraf, advanced toward Shiraz, but their relations were uneasy—any alliance between Chupani and Inju could not last very long. When their combined forces had made camp at Ja'farabad north of Shiraz, Abu Eshaq entered the city and shut out Malek Ashraf. The Shirazis took up arms in support of Abu Eshaq, attacked Malek Ashraf's camp by night, and scattered the Chupani forces. At the same time Mas'ud Shah, apparently unaware of the progress of his younger brother, also returned to Shiraz with the support of Amir Yaghi Basti b. Amir Chupan (Malek Ashraf's uncle), one of Sheikh Hasan-e-Bozorg's commanders. Abu Eshaq yielded to his older brother's claim and withdrew eastward to the Shabankareh district.[23]

But coexistence between an Inju ruler (Mas'ud Shah) and a Chupani commander (Yaghi Basti) was as impossible in 1342 as it had been three years earlier between Amir Mohammad and Pir Hosein. Yaghi Basti could not endure being Mas'ud Shah's deputy and guest in Shiraz, and in 1342 Yaghi Basti's men murdered Jalal al-Din Mas'ud Shah as he left the bath.

Round Five: The Last Inju Left Standing Seizes Shiraz

Abu Eshaq, now the last surviving son of Mahmud Shah Inju, moved to avenge his brother's death. A group of Shirazi nobles, neighborhood chiefs, guild-masters, and street mob leaders joined forces to support Abu Eshaq. Attacking Yaghi Basti, they forced him into the governor's residence. Gangs supporting the rival claimants brawled in the streets for twenty days until the ruler of Kazeroun intervened on Abu Eshaq's side and drove Yaghi Basti and his men from the city.

The Last Round: The Final Chupani Counterattack Fails

After this defeat the Chupanis made a last attempt to take Shiraz. In the following year, 1343, Yaghi Basti and his nephew Malek Ashraf joined forces and marched on the city. With the help of Mohammad Mozaffar they captured Abarqu and slaughtered the inhabitants, but news of the gruesome death of the head of the Chupani family, Sheikh Hasan-e-Kuchek (see p. 29), stopped their advance. The two Chupanis immediately returned to Tabriz, while Mohammad Mozaffar returned to Yazd.[24]

Thus in 1343, Jamal al-Din Shah Sheikh Abu Eshaq held undisputed control of Fars, the Persian Gulf coast, and Esfahan, with no rival claimants from either his own family or the Chupanis. He had advanced from being a vassal *amir* to being a *soltan,* with coins struck and the Friday sermon read in his name. Along with the Mozaffarids in Yazd and Kerman, the Jalayerids (or Ilkanids) in Iraq and Kurdestan, the Sarbedarids around Sabzevar in western Khorasan, the Chupanids in Azarbaijan, and the Kurts (or Karts) in Herat and Northeastern Iran, he now ruled one of the six successor kingdoms to the Il-Khanid state.

CONCLUSION: A VIOLENT SETTING

As the poet Shams al-Din Mohammad Hafez was growing up in Shiraz, he witnessed the murderous violence and strife of his time—he may well have participated in it. He was a young man in his twenties when the rule of Fars changed hands *eight times* between 1339 and 1344, when factional strife claimed three of the four sons of Mahmud Shah Inju, and when Chupanid and Mozaffarid armies massacred the entire population of Abarqu.

Although Shiraz escaped destruction at the hands of the Mongols, their rule still brought anarchy, violence, and severe economic hardship. Earlier rulers of Shiraz, harsh as they were, had shown some concern for the well-being of their subjects, who were the basis of the rulers' armies and incomes. In the late thirteenth and early fourteenth centuries, except in isolated instances, even that concern disappeared—and Shiraz suffered the general fate of plunder at the hands of Turco-Mongol military rulers who seemed interested only in grabbing loot as quickly as possible, and who usually despised the settled traditions of Iranian life.

3

Shiraz as City-State: Abu Eshaq Inju and the Mozaffarids

راستی خاتم فیروزه بو اسحاقی   خوش درخشید ولی دولت مستعجل بود

Truly, the Abu Eshaq turquoise ring
Dazzled, but with only an ephemeral shine.

—*Hafez*

Contemporaries such as the historian Zarkub and the poet Hafez praised Abu Eshaq Inju for his intelligence, bravery, chivalry, and generosity. After surviving the bloody struggles described in the previous chapter, he took control of Fars and Esfahan, and held them for eleven years. Poets and historians have memorialized him as a lover of art, literature, and religious scholarship, and his brief reign saw brilliant achievements in all those fields.

His character had a dark and erratic side as well. He provoked disastrous wars with Mohammad Mozaffar, who had begun his career as little more than a local warlord and road guardian in a subdistrict of Yazd. Abu Eshaq also had a destructive mistrust of the Shirazis, who had long supported his family against rivals, particularly the Chupanis. At crucial times, such as during Mohammad Mozaffar's siege of Shiraz in 1352–53, Abu Eshaq would withdraw into depression, inaction, suspicion, and debauchery.

By 1343, Abu Eshaq had achieved undisputed control of Fars. When he attempted to reestablish his authority in Kerman, however, he came into conflict with the Amir Mobarez al-Din Mohammad Mozaffar of Yazd, who had taken the province from Abu Eshaq's father during the multi-sided conficts described earlier.[1] The two rulers probably could have made peace, but the young "Shah Sheikh" decided to regain family territory by force and to seek revenge for Amir Mohammad's alliance with the hated Chupanis.

In 1345 Abu Eshaq made two unsuccessful expeditions against Kerman, one of which resulted in the death of his minister Shams al-Din Sa'en Qazi Semnani. The next year saw Abu Eshaq stirring up the Mongol tribes of Kerman against Amir Mohammad. He repeatedly attacked both Yazd and Kerman, but his campaigns were costly failures. His last attack on Yazd in 1350 led to a protracted siege during which the inhabitants were reduced to cannibalism. He made his last unsuccessful attack on Kerman in 1352, losing many of his generals in the fiasco.

Abu Eshaq squandered his wealth on these losing campaigns—a mistake which eventually caused his own downfall. Following his last victory outside Kerman, Amir Mohammad Mozaffar used his captured booty to take the offensive against Abu Eshaq in Shiraz.[2] First naming his son Shah Shoja as his successor, Amir Mohammad gathered troops from the Arab and Mongol tribes of Kerman and from the forces of his son Sharaf al-Din Mozaffar in Yazd. These forces assembled on the plains of Arzaviyeh, southwest of Kerman. When Abu Eshaq learned of the coming attack, he sent, on the recommendation of his advisors, the scholar Mowlana Azod al-Din Abd al-Rahman Iji on a peace mission. Amir Mohammad treated the Inju ambassador with great respect, but would not be dissuaded from attacking Shiraz. He told Azod al-Din that Abu Eshaq had broken eight peace agreements and that now only war could decide the issues between them.[3]

With Amir Mohammad advancing on Shiraz from the southeast, Abu Eshaq withdrew into passivity and drink. He led his forces to Pol-e-Fasa, about fifteen miles southeast of Shiraz, but, exhausted and with no will to fight, he withdrew into the city without meeting the attacking Mozaffarids. Throughout the six-month siege of Shiraz, Abu Eshaq remained seemingly unaware of the dangers threatening him. He retreated further into drunkenness and suspicion and let control of the city pass into the hands of neighborhood mob leaders. Once, in a drunken stupor, he heard the drums of the besieging army and asked, "What is that noise?" When he learned it was the kettledrums of Amir Mohammad, he said, "You mean that stubborn fellow is still here?"[4]

Amir Mohammad Mozaffar was everything Abu Eshaq was not: austere, ruthless, and determined. He inherited courage from his father, who, fifty years before, killed a Mongol officer in Shiraz who forced his way into a women's bath. During the siege of Shiraz, Amir Mohammad responded to a rebellion of an ally, Majd al-Din Bandamiri, by storming the rebel's fortress and slaughtering his whole family, including his seven-year-old son (whom Amir Mohammad executed personally). Neither the death of his own eldest son nor a painful illness during the siege of Shiraz could make Amir Mohammad abandon his assault on the Injus.

In the end, Abu Eshaq lost Shiraz more by his own ineptitude than to Mozaffarid attacks. Abu Eshaq owed his position and his very life to the support of the Shirazi *pahlavanan* (popular heroes) and *kaluviyan* (bazaar and neighborhood chiefs) who controlled the town mobs.[5] He had attempted to free himself from their influence, realizing that they could challenge his authority, shift their support to his enemies, and drive him out just as they had earlier driven out the Chupani rulers. In 1344 a Shirazi *rend* (street ruffian) killed one of Abu Eshaq's ministers, and the ruler, in an effort to control this unruly population, disarmed the Shirazis and appointed only Esfahanis as his close advisors. As for the patricians of Shiraz, they remained torn between their fear of popular rebellion and their links with the neighborhood leaders.[6]

During the siege of 1352–53, Abu Eshaq's mistrust of the Shirazis led him to make a fatal mistake. He executed the chief of the *seyyeds* in the *Masjed-e-Now* area and the chief of the important *Bagh-e-Now* quarter after accusing them of collaborating with the besieging Mozaffarids. Abu Eshaq also made plans to execute Kalu Omar, the son of the chief of the western *Murdestan* quarter. When Kalu Omar discovered Abu Eshaq's intentions, he began doing what the ruler suspected, and made secret contact with Amir Mohammad.

During the siege, Abu Eshaq lost two of his key advisors and supporters. One was Haji Qavam al-Din Hasan Tamghachi, who died in 1353. Qavam al-Din had served the Inju family for twenty-five years, and had earned, by his generosity, the respect of all classes and the praises of the

poet Hafez, the historian Zarkub, and others.[7] Abu Eshaq also lost the
support of Mowlana Azod al-Din Iji (the unsuccessful peace envoy to Amir
Mohammad), who joined the besieging forces after he persuaded one of
the city's *kaluviyan* to let him leave Shiraz through the Kazeroun Gate.

Abu Eshaq's alienating Shirazi neighborhood chiefs was his downfall.
The inhabitants of the Murdestan quarter were responsible for the defense
of the Beiza Gate on the western side of the city. Shah Shoja Mozaffari
received a message from Kalu Omar, the son of the neighborhood chief,
that he was ready to open the gate to the besieging forces. As the Mozaffarid
armies made diversionary attacks elsewhere, Amir Mohammad led his men
into the city through the open western gate. Abu Eshaq, unable to resist
further, fled west with a few followers and shut himself in the Qal'eh-ye-
Sefid stronghold.

THE INSPECTOR RULES SHIRAZ

The Shirazis now found themselves under a very different sort of ruler.
Amir Mohammad first treated Abu Eshaq's associates well, but later killed
a number of them, including his ten-year-old son and Kalu Fakhr al-Din,
chief of the Kazeroun Gate district and one of Abu Eshaq's most important supporters among the neighborhood chiefs. On the pretext of
reforming the *owqaf* (pious endowments) of Shiraz, Amir Mohammad
confiscated most of them and converted them to government property.
He improved urban security by controlling the street mobs. Unlike the
easygoing Abu Eshaq, he was very strict in religious matters, enjoining
the people to listen to *hadith* (traditions of the prophet), *tafsir* (Koranic
commentary), and *feqh* (jurisprudence) and to follow closely the dictates
of religion, avoiding any taint of depravity (*fesq va fojur*).

These actions earned Amir Mohammad the nickname of *mohtaseb* (cen-
sor, inspector) among the Shirazis. When he closed the pleasure-lovers'
favorite haunts—the wine shops, opium houses, and brothels—Hafez
described the times in some of his most famous verses.

اگر باده فرح بخش و باد گلبیزست   ببانگ چنگ مخور می که محتسب تیزست

در آستین مرقع پیاله پنهان کن   که همچو چشم صراحی زمانه خونریزست

ز رنگ باده بشوئید خرقه ها از اشک   که موسم ورع و روزگار پرهیزست

Though wine gives delight and wind distills the perfume
  of the rose,
Drink not wine to the strains of the harp, for the inspector
  is awake.
Hide the goblet in the sleeve of the patchwork cloak,
For the times, like the eye of the decanter, pour forth blood.
Wash the wine-stain from your dervish-cloak with tears,
For it is the season of piety and the time of abstinence.

and:

بود آیا که در میکده ها بگشایند   گره از کار فرو بستۀ ما بگشایند

در میخانه بستند خدایا مپسند   که در خانۀ تزویر و ریا بگشایند

اگر از بهر دل زاهد خود بین بستند   دل قوی دار که از بهر خدا بگشایند

O, when will they open the doors of the taverns
And untie the knots of our tangled affairs?
They have closed the tavern doors. O God, don't let
Them open the doors of the house of deceit and hypocrisy.
If they have closed them for the sake of the selfish ascetic,
Be strong, for they will reopen them for the sake of God.

Even Amir Mohammad's son, Shah Shoja, joined the critics and composed verses about his father's strict rule. He also dissuaded his father from
destroying the tomb of the poet Sa'adi. Amir Mohammad had objected
to Sa'adi's verses on religious grounds, but Shah Shoja persuaded him that
the poet had repented in the verse

سعدیا بسیار گفتن عمر ضایع کردن است   وقت عذر آوردن استغفرالله العظیم

O Sa'adi, speaking too much is a waste of your life.
Now is the time of repentance and [saying] "God forbid."

As Amir Mohammad pursued the fleeing Abu Eshaq, his sons suppressed
scattered revolts against Mozaffarid authority. His son Mahmud Shah cap-

tured Ij, the capital of the Shabankareh, brought the area under direct rule, and ended a tribal dynasty that had originated over three centuries earlier during the Buyid era.[8]

A year after taking Shiraz the Mozaffarids lost the city briefly to an Inju counterattack. While Amir Mohammad moved against Abu Eshaq in Esfahan, he put his nephew Shah Sultan in Shiraz and his son Shah Shoja in Kerman. With the main Mozaffarid forces moving against Esfahan, Abu Eshaq's supporters from Shulestan, the remote region northeast of Kazeroun, attacked Shiraz, where the pro-Inju inhabitants of the Kazeroun Gate district let the attacking forces into the city. Shah Sultan's men were caught by surprise, and the Shulestanis and their Shirazi allies looted the governor's palace and attacked the pro-Mozaffarid Murdestan quarter.[9] When Shah Shoja and his forces entered Shiraz through the (northern) Estakhr gate, the two armies fought a full-scale street battle that ended in the defeat of the Inju partisans. The inhabitants of the Kazeroun Gate area and their Shulestani allies, however, continued to fight until their neighborhood was completely destroyed.

In 1357 the Mozaffarid armies captured Abu Eshaq at Esfahan and sent him as a prisoner to Amir Mohammad at Shiraz. There, before the assembled judges and nobles of the city, Amir Mohammad delivered Abu Eshaq for execution to Amir Qotb al-Din, the son of a Seyyed earlier executed by Abu Eshaq. Just before his execution Abu Eshaq recited the following verses:

افسوس که مرغ عمر را دانه نماند   وامید بهیچ خویش و بیگانه نماند

دردا و دریغا که در این مدت عمر   از هر چه بگفتیم جز افسانه نماند

Alas that no grain remains for the bird of life,
Alas that no hope is left from family or stranger.
Alas that from this span of our life,
Nothing I have said remains but stories.

Having secured his rule in Fars, Shabankareh, Kerman, Lorestan, and Esfahan, Amir Mohammad now embarked on more ambitious conquests. In

1357 he marched on Azarbaijan, which had been in anarchy since the death of Malek Ashraf Chupani that same year. In 1358 Amir Mohammad captured Tabriz, and on his first Friday there he mounted the pulpit and personally read the Friday sermon in the name of the Abbasid caliph of Egypt.[10] At the approach of a Jalayerid army under Sultan Oveis b. Sheikh Hasan Bozorg, however, Amir Mohammad abandoned Tabriz after a two-month occupation and retreated to Esfahan.

THE INSPECTOR CHOKES ON HIS OWN BILE

During this campaign Amir Mohammad brought his own downfall by his suspicious nature and harsh temper. He had terrified both his sons and his nephew, cursing them publicly and threatening them with arrest, blinding, and execution.[11] In 1358, while returning from Tabriz to Esfahan, Amir Mohammad's two sons and his nephew arrested him and killed his minister. They blinded Amir Mohammad himself and confined him in the notorious *Qal'eh-ye-Sefid* in Fars. Even in his blindness, however, Amir Mohammad continued to fight, and within a few months had tricked the fortress-keeper into turning over the castle to him. Eventually Amir Mohammad pretended to be reconciled with his sons, who allowed him and his household to live in Shiraz and rule as a figurehead. The obstinate Mozaffarid, however, still sought revenge, and plotted with another of his sons to kill Shah Shoja. The latter discovered the plot, killed the conspirators, and once again imprisoned his father, this time in the unhealthy *Qal'eh-ye-Tabar*. The castle's hot climate and salty water undermined the health of Amir Mohammad, who died there in 1364.

The Mozaffarid family (see table 3.1) was best known for its feuds, beginning with the blinding of Amir Mohammad and ending only with the final destruction of the dynasty by Timur in 1393. During the long reign of Shah Shoja (r. 1358–84) the Mozaffarid realm reached its greatest extent, but the ruler was never free of family squabbling. During these years the Mozaffarids controlled Khuzestan, Lorestan, and Baluchestan, in addition to their core possessions of Fars, Kerman, and Esfahan. In 1375 they held Azarbaijan and Arran briefly, but, because of internal divisions, had to abandon this area after a four-month occupation.

In 1359 Shah Shoja made Shiraz his capital, and made one brother, Shah Mahmud, ruler of Esfahan and Abarqu, and another brother, Sultan

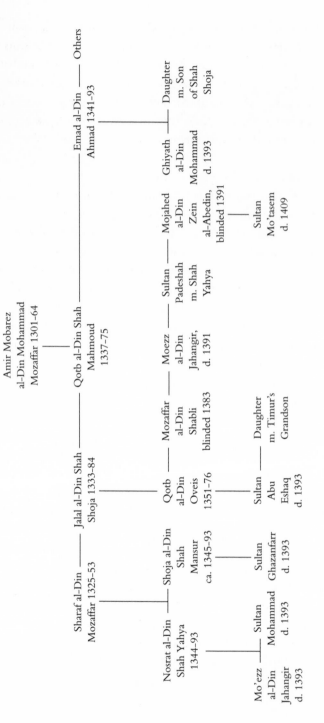

Table 3.1. Some of the Mozaffarids

Ahmad, ruler of Kerman. He imprisoned his nephew Shah Yahya in Fahan-dezh castle near Shiraz until the two made peace in 1363, when Shah Yahya swore allegiance to his uncle and became governor of Yazd. During his reign Shah Shoja fought continuously with both his brother Shah Mah-mud and his nephew Shah Yahya. During these struggles Shiraz came under attack numerous times and fell into Shah Mahmud's hands from 1364 to 1366. As often as the two brothers made peace, they broke their agree-ments. Shah Shoja enjoyed the secret support of his brother's wife, Khan Sultan of the Inju family.[12] For his part, Shah Mahmud allied himself with the Jalayerid rulers of Baghdad. The fratricide ended only with the death of Shah Mahmud in 1375.

Shah Mahmud's death, however, did not end the battles among the Mozaffarids. Shah Shoja continued to fight with his nephew Shah Yahya in Yazd and with Yahya's brother Shah Mansur, who, with Jalayerid sup-port, established himself as independent ruler in Shushtar. In 1383, in a fit of drunkenness and suspicion, Shah Shoja ordered his men to blind his own son, Sultan Shebli. The following day Shah Shoja repented of his action, but too late.

After the blinding of his son came a series of disasters for Shah Shoja. He lost his mother, Makhdum Shah, and his nephew Shah Hosein (brother of Shah Yahya and Shah Mansur). Shah Shoja himself fell into a fatal illness as a result of drunken orgies at Shiraz. On his deathbed he appointed his son Zein al-Abedin as successor and warned him to avoid family conflicts and preserve unity. He appointed his brother Abu Yazid ruler of Esfahan, his nephew Shah Yahya ruler of Yazd, and another brother, Sultan Emad al-Din Ahmad, ruler of Kerman.

The dying Shah Shoja also sent letters to Amir Timur and to the Jalay-erid ruler, entrusting his heirs to their care.[13] Shah Shoja had realized that his family could not resist the growing power of Timur, and, during Timur's second campaign in northeastern Iran in 1382, sent the conqueror an envoy with rich gifts and promises of loyalty. Timur received the Mozaffarid ambassador kindly, and sent his own envoy to Shiraz to bring a bride from Shah Shoja's family. Two years later, the two families made a marriage alliance between Shah Shoja's granddaughter and Amir Timur's grand-son. Shah Shoja himself died in 1384 at the age of 53. His tomb still exists in Shiraz, adjacent to the Haft-Tan complex, with a stone from the eigh-teenth century and a modest twentieth-century dome.

THE END OF THE MOZAFFARIDS

Events in Shiraz following the death of Shah Shoja resembled those following the death of the Salghurid Atabek Abu Bakr b. Sa'd over a century before.[14] In both cases a strong-willed ruler of a quarrelsome minor dynasty had preserved his independence by able diplomacy and by timely submission to superior outside force—in one case, to the Mongols, and in another to the Timurids. In both cases the death of that ruler led to a free-for-all among his successors, which ended only when the powerful outside conqueror intervened, eliminated the dynasty, and established direct rule.

The squabbling Mozaffarid princes ignored Shah Shoja's advice to stand united. The nine years from Shah Shoja's death in 1384 to the family's final destruction in 1393 was a period of complex moves and counter-moves involving major and minor family members, their military commanders, tribal leaders, Sultan Ahmad Jalayeri, and Amir Timur himself. Timur first occupied Shiraz in 1387 and appointed Shah Yahya as vassal ruler. In 1393 Timur defeated Shah Mansur, occupied Shiraz again, and divided the Mozaffarid territory among Timurid officers. Timur appointed his own son Omar Sheikh to be ruler of Shiraz and replaced the Mozaffarid princes, who had been ruling the other cities of southern Iran, with his own appointees.[15]

During his second occupation of Shiraz, Timur put an end to the struggles of this contentious family. He summoned to Shiraz all of the Mozaffarid princes, who, out of fear or out of hope of returning to power, dared not disobey.[16] Timur at first treated the Mozaffarids with respect, but later arrested all of them except the two blinded sons of Shah Shoja and one of his grandsons. In 1393, when Timur left Shiraz, he took the Mozaffarid princes and the city's artists, scholars, and craftsmen with him. The latter group he took to his capital at Samarqand, but murdered the princes before they could reach Esfahan.

MOZAFFARID AND INJU REMAINS

The Mozaffarids have earned reflected glory from the praise of contemporary poets such as Hafez, Obeid Zakani, Faqih Emad al-Din Kermani, Khaju Kermani, and others. But in Shiraz itself little remains from this family's rule. The Mozaffarids were more attached to Kerman, Yazd, and

Esfahan, and did most of their building in those cities. Mozaffarid remains in Shiraz are few, and survive in buildings, inscriptions, and names of urban quarters.

The mother of Shah Shoja, Khatun Qotlogh Beg, endowed a complex of buildings in the Bahaliyeh district near the Beiza (western) Gate. This complex included a school, the domed tomb of Seyyedeh Omm Abdallah Bibi Dokhtaran (of unknown date), and the tomb of the Khatun herself, who died in 1383. In 1972 only the domed tomb, without decoration or inscription, survived.[17]

Traces of the graves of two Mozaffarid rulers still remain. Shah Shoja is buried on the slopes of the Chehel Maqam north of the city, adjoining the Haft-tan garden. A modest modern inscription marks the site. Shah Mansur's grave is near the present Sa'adi Gate, in the eastern part of the city in an area today called Gowd-e-Shahzadeh Mansur (Prince Mansur's Tomb).

In 1969 the author found a piece of a dated dedication inscription (p. 44) for a mosque founded by a "Hosein Esmail" in 1385. This inscription, in excellent condition, was unearthed in 1969 next to Abesh Khatun's tomb southeast of the modern city. No trace, however, remains of the Dar al-Shafa Seminary, founded by Shah Shoja in the Dashtak (Sar-e-Dozak) quarter, south of the Old Congregational Mosque, probably on the site of the tenth-century Buyid hospital of the same name. The school survived only as a name in the sources and in the name of its district.[18]

The most famous son of Shiraz died at the end of the Mozaffarid period. The tomb of the poet Hafez (d. 1389) in the Mosalla district is today one of the city's most popular pilgrimage sites, where visitors seek advice and prophecy from the poet's verses. The present tomb and garden, known as Hafeziyeh, dates from the 1930s.

The Inju ruler Shah Sheikh Abu Eshaq was more generous to Shiraz. Outside the city gates he began the construction of an imitation of the famous Sassanian Taq-e-Kisra at Ctesiphon. This building was never completed and no trace survives.[19] Abu Eshaq also built what is still the most exquisite historical building in Shiraz—the *khoda khaneh* or the *dar al-masahef* (Qoran library) of the Old Congregational Mosque. This library, built in the middle of the mosque court-yard, originally contained Qorans in the handwriting of the companions of the prophets, and one written

INSCRIPTION FROM A MOSQUE
FOUNDATION

by the third Caliph Othman, with bloodstains from his assassination on
its pages. This building, restored in 1941, has an inscription around its top
in fine *sols* script which dates the building to 1351.[20]

Other Inju buildings, some of which survive only as names in the
sources, include:

> The rebuilt dome of the mausoleum of Seyyed Ahmad b. Musa (Shah-
> e-Cheragh) and a school, the Madraseh-ye-Tashi, adjoining the
> shrine. Tashi Khatun, the mother of Shah Abu Eshaq, endowed both
> of these projects.

> The Madraseh-ye-Mas'udiyeh (location unknown) founded by Jalal
> al-Din Mas'ud Shah, brother of Abu Eshaq.

> The rebuilt tomb of Sheikh Abu Bakr Allaf (a companion of Ibn
> Khafif Sheikh al-Kabir, d. 990) in the Darb-e-Estakhr quarter (the
> present-day Bazar-e-Vakil). Haji Qavam al-Din Hasan, Abu Eshaq's
> minister, endowed this project.

The tomb of the poet Khaju Kermani (d. 1352), now located in a small garden in the Allahu Akbar Gorge north of the city.

The tomb of Sheikh Baba al-Din Ali b. Abu Bakr Badal (d. 1338). This grave is in the Darb-b-Estakhr quarter and in 1972 still existed in a corner of the yard of Shahpour High School.

Another monument of this period lies forgotten, deep in the old city in the area between the Old Congregational Mosque and the shrine of Hosein b. Musa (modern Astaneh). The inhabitants today call this small shrine Panj-tan (Five Saints). It is probably the mausoleum of the Zarkubs, the family of the author of the fourteenth-century Shiraznameh. This shrine includes the graves of the historian's ancestors, dating to the thirteenth century C.E., of his brother, and of the historian himself, Mo'in al-Din Ahmad b. Abu al-Kheir, who died in 1387.[21]

PART TWO

City of Roses and Nightingales

4

Peoples and Places

صفاهونم صفاهونم چه جائی   که هر یاری گرفتم بی وفائی
شوم یک سر برونم تا به شیراز که در هر منزلم صد آشنائی

> *Esfahan, Esfahan, what a place!*
> *Where every lover is faithless.*
> *Straight to Shiraz will I flee,*
> *And a hundred friends find at every stop.*
>
> *—Baba Taher*

The poet Shams al-Din Mohammad Hafez Shirazi (ca. 1320–1389) lived through decades of bloodshed and anarchy in his native city. If his Shiraz was a place of violence, however, it was also a place of piety, scholarship, and artistic genius. While rulers, generals, and ministers played their deadly power games, there was just enough prosperity and stability for Hafez to compose his magnificent lyrics, probably unequalled before or since. Alongside the Shirazi poet, the merchant in the bazaar, the preacher in the mosque, the judge and scholar in the seminary, the artist in his workshop, and the sufi in his retreat were busy creating a rich, varied cultural and economic life that could weather the city's frequent, intense storms of political violence.

THE HUMAN SETTING
Like all Iranian cities, Shiraz has experienced alternating periods of stagnation and prosperity. In 1972, among the provincial cities of Iran, it had fallen behind the industrial centers of Esfahan and Tabriz and the great religious center of Mashhad. At that time, before the upsets of the Islamic

Revolution and the 1980–88 Iran-Iraq war, Shiraz enjoyed a modest prosperity from its university, its military installations, and its tourism, despite
the fact that trade routes between the Persian Gulf and the interior had
shifted away from its traditional port of Bushehr. As the photograph on
page 5 shows, a modern town of straight, wide avenues and spacious houses
had grown up north and west of the old city. The old city sat on the site
of the original Shiraz founded in the first century of Islam. Although the
city's center had shifted to the newly built avenues of the modern town,
the old city had never been abandoned and continued to exist side-by-side
with modern Shiraz.[1]

Area and Population

We can estimate the population of fourteenth-century Shiraz by calcu-
lating its area and likely population density, and by scattered accounts in
the sources. According to one Venetian traveler, in the fifteenth century
Shiraz was about thirty kilometers in circumference and had a population of 200,000. Both figures are overestimates, but take more meaning
when combined with a second Venetian traveler's statement that Shiraz
and its suburbs were thirty kilometers in circumference. Combining the
two accounts, it is reasonable to say that Shiraz and its suburbs (including
the land north of the city between the Dry River and the mountains) had
a circumference of about twenty miles and the (larger) region *(mantaqeh,
boluk)* of Shiraz had a population of about 200,000.[2]

The exact boundaries of the fourteenth-century city could not have
been very different from those of Zand and Qajar Shiraz in the eighteenth
and nineteenth centuries. The aerial photograph on page 5 shows the clear
demarcation between the modern and old cities—a demarcation that also
represents the boundary of the nineteenth-century (Qajar) town. The only
important differences between these later boundaries and those of the fourteenth century occurred at the northwest and southeast corners of Shiraz,
where the extent of the city in the fourteenth century is uncertain.

The circumference of the fourteenth-century city was between seven
and eight kilometers, and its area between 350 and 390 hectares. We can
estimate the population at about 50–60,000. Assuming that about one-
fourth of the region's population lived in Shiraz itself, the earlier figure
of 200,000 becomes a reasonable estimate for the population of the entire
Shiraz area.[3]

The People

The inhabitants of Shiraz spoke a variety of languages, including Persian, Turkish, Lori, and Arabic. Sheikh Ruzbehan Baqli (d. 1209) composed verses in the Shirazi dialect of his time. Both the language and the content of the following verses, for example, are similar to that of the present-day folk poetry of Fars.[4]

> Yekesh va kowk o baz khowshen
> Yekesh va zohd o navaz khowshen
> Meski del-e-Ruzbehan
> Kesh va yek raz khowshen

> One is happy with quails and hawks;
> Another is happy with holy poverty and prayers.
> Have pity on the heart of poor Ruzbehan
> Which is happy with only one secret.

and

> Veh bad-e-qahr-e-to shakh-e-omid-e-ma nashkest
> Aru ke tot aneh bikh-e-vojud-e-ma resheh-hen

> The wind of your scorn could not break the branch of my hope,
> For you are rooted in the base of my existence.

The *Divan* of the famous poet of food, Mowlana Boshaq Hallaj Shirazi Sheikh At'ameh (d. 1436), also contains verses in dialect. Some verses, such as the following, combine colloquial and literary Persian:

مزعفر قند و مرغش میبرازه   دل روغن ز مهرش میگدازه

> Its saffron-sugar and its birds are comely.
> It melts the heart of the oil by its kindness.

Fourteenth-century Shiraz also contained a Jewish community speaking its own dialect and writing Persian in Hebrew characters. We have already noted the presence of a large Zoroastrian community in Shiraz during the Buyid period, but by the time of Hafez four centuries later, it survived only as a convention in his poetry with its references to Zoroastrian priests (*mogh,* pl. *moghan*) and in expressions such as *kharabat-e-moghan* (tavern), *pir-e-moghan* (tavern-keeper), and *mogh-bachcheh* (tavern-keeper's boy). The drink-shops of Hafez's time would have been in the hands of other non-Moslems, either Jews or Christians.

Iranian genius, of whatever faith, has always expressed itself best in poetry. Accordingly the Jews of Shiraz in this period produced their greatest poet, Mowlana Shahin Shirazi. Mowlana Shahin put the Pentateuch into Persian verse (in Hebrew script) under the title *Musa-Nameh,* in imitation of the Iranian epic *Shahnameh.* His work occupied thirty years and, according to his own account, was completed in 1359.[5]

Most of the city's population consisted of native Shirazis and persons who had migrated from the other districts of Fars.[6] Fourteenth-century scholars in Shiraz also came from more distant origins, bearing names indicating both Deilamite (e.g. Banjir, Bakalanjar, and Kalijar) and Turkish origin. Although the violence in most of Iran during the thirteenth and fourteenth centuries must have caused migrations to relatively safe areas such as Fars, these migrations remained mostly individual rather than mass movements.[7]

Among the most famous immigrant scholars was Sheikh Zahir al-Din Abd al-Rahman b. Ali (d. 1316), the teacher of Ahmad Zarkub (author of the *Shiraznameh*). Sheikh Zahir was the grandson of a Turkish merchant named Bozghash who settled in Shiraz in the Salghurid era. Another scholar of Turkish origin was Sheikh Sarraj al-Din Joneid (d. 1379), the son of Sheikh Turan b. Abdullah Turki. According to the account in *Shadd al-Izar,* Sheikh Turan had been a Turkish soldier who renounced warfare for piety; his sons then became renowned scholars. In addition to Turkish and Deilamite names, Hafez's Shiraz contained scholars whose *nesbat*s related them to Esfahan, Khorasan, Ardabil, Semnan, Qazvin, Samarqand, Khojand, and even Egypt.[8]

THE PHYSICAL SETTING

Shiraz did not have a city wall until 1044, when the insecurity of the late Buyid period forced Abu Kalijar Deilami to build a wall 12,500 paces in circumference.[9] During the following centuries, the wall fell into ruin and rulers repaired it numerous times. In 1302 the Mongol ruler Ghazan Khan ordered it completely rebuilt and had a moat added at a cost of five tomans (50,000 dinars) in gold. During the fourteenth century, constant warfare forced rulers to pay close attention to the condition of the wall. Mahmud Shah Inju in 1325 and Shah Shoja in 1366 ordered repairs on the wall and its towers.[10] In 1972 no trace of the walls and gates of Shiraz remained, except in names of places like Darvazeh Kazeroun and Darvazeh Esfahan. Memories of the city walls also lingered in such names as Kal-e-Moshir and Kal-e-Teimuri, where *kal* in Shirazi dialect refers to a gap or ruined space in a wall.

According to Mostowfi, in 1340 Shiraz had nine gates.[11] Although the gates themselves have long disappeared, some can be located. These gates were:

Estakhr Gate: on the north side of the city, in an area called the Esfahan Gate in 1972.

Darak Musa Gate: exact location unknown, probably on the west side of the city opposite the Darak Mountain.

Beiza Gate: on the west side of the city adjoining the Murdestan quarter and near the eighth/fourteenth-century mausoleum of Bibi Dokhtaran. In the nineteenth century this gate was called Darb-e-Bagh-e-Shah.

Kazeroun Gate: at the southwest corner of the city, in an area of the same name.

Salam or Salm Gate: on the south side of the city opposite the Dar al-Salam cemetery. In 1972 this area was called the Shah Dai Gate.

Fasa Gate: on the southeast edge of the city. In the tenth century this gate was called the Kavar Gate (from the small town on the road to Firuzabad) and in 1972 it was known as the Qassabkhaneh (Slaughterhouse) Gate.

Now (New) Gate: location unknown, probably on the east side of the city. *Shadd al-Izar* mentions the Bagh-e-Now Gate adjoining a district of the same name.

Dowlat Gate: exact location unknown, on the eastern or northeastern side of the city adjoining the Bagh-e-Now district. Named for Sheikh Dowlat b. Ebrahim, a warrior killed in battle with the Zoroastrians of Fahandezh at the time of the Arab conquest.

Sa'adat Gate: location unknown.

Urban Quarters

> *After a bottle of araq, no one in Sar-e-Dozak would dare challenge him.*
> —*Sadegh Hedayat, "Dash Akol"*

The city quarters played a key role in the political struggles of the fourteenth century by supporting one or another of the princes competing for power. According to Mostowfi, in 1340 Shiraz had seventeen quarters *(mahalleh)*, which he does not name. The author of *Shadd al-Izar*, writing about 1389, divides the city into seven areas *(nowbat)* for pilgrimage to the graves of saints, corresponding to days of the week.[12] There was no orderly system of nomenclature for larger or smaller units. Quarters were divided into smaller areas, which might be called *mahalleh, mahal, kucheh,* or *ku*.

Urban areas might take their names from former villages absorbed into the city, or for some important site in the area—a bazaar, a mosque, a seminary, a city gate, a saint's tomb, or a garden. A typical Shiraz address could be as follows: Kazeroun Gate district; behind the Bahar bath house; in the Kucheh-ye-Qazi; opposite the mosque of the Darabis; the home of Haji Ja'far Khabbaz.

Table 4.1 (pp. 56–57) shows the geography of Hafez's Shiraz by reconstructing the layout of its quarters and districts.[13] A family would often take the name of a city district as all or part of its *nesbat*. Thus, the author of the biographical work *Shadd al-Izar* was Mo'in al-Din Joneid b. Mahmud b. Mohammad *Baghnovi*. The author's ancestor Zein al-Din Mozaffar (d. 1206) first used the *nesbat* Baghnovi when he migrated from Fasa to Shiraz, and settled, and was later buried, in the Bagh-e-Now district. The author of the nineteenth-century *Farsnameh-ye-Naseri,* Haj Mirza Hasan Fasa'i, traced his ancestry to the family of the Dashtaki-Shirazi Seyyeds, who took their name from the Dashtak district, south of the Old Congregational Mosque. From the early fourteenth century this family, originally known as Arabshah-Hoseini, built its family tombs and endowed a seminary in that same neighborhood. Eventually the name of this district became part of the family *nesbat.*

Water Supply

The lifeblood of any city of the Iranian plateau is its water supply. Shiraz needed water both for domestic use and for the extensive agricultural areas surrounding the city. That water came from underground channels (*qanats*) and one spring. In 1327, Ibn Battuta noted that five streams (presumably fed by *qanats*) passed through the city.[14] The best-known water source was the Ab-e-Rokni, built by the Buyid Rokn al-Dowleh in 950, which flowed into the city from the north through the Allahu Akbar defile. The best water came from the Zangi Qanat, constructed by the Salghurid Atabek Zangi b. Mowdud in 1165 about two miles east of the city. The most plentiful water supply came from the Fahandezh or Sa'adi Qanat, a few miles northeast of the city. It supplied (and still supplied in 1972) water for the village around the tomb of Sa'adi and for the farms on the plains around the mountain of Zaijan.[15] The only important spring of Shiraz was the Cheshmeh-ye-Jushak, about eight miles northwest of the city, which irrigated the gardens and farms of the present Masjed-Bardi area.

Rulers and other wealthy benefactors would endow public fountains (*saqayeh*) fed by these underground channels.[16] Mosques and baths needed large amounts of fresh water for their pools—in summer the courtyard of the Old Congregational Mosque was washed every evening. Some houses also had private wells, which would be useful during sieges and disturbances.

Rainwater and melting snow from Darak Musa Mountain flowed into the salt lake of Maharlu east of Shiraz through the seasonal Khoshk River, which ran outside the northern wall of the city. This river provided natural flood control in the spring and during periods of heavy rain. Although the fourteenth-century sources praise Shiraz for its good water and its cleanliness, the waste disposal system, according to Mostowfi, left much to be desired.[17]

Table 4.1. Geography of Shiraz

14th Century Pilgrimage Area	Location	14th Century Quarters Known	Unknown
Sheikh-e-Kabir	Northern part of city: 1972 bazaar area	Darb-e-Estakhr	Namdar Sepidan
Bahaliyeh	Southwest part of city	Darvazeh-Kazeroun Darb-e-Masjed-Now, Murdestan	Qazi Sokhtoviyeh
Dar al-Salm	Outside southern wall	Uninhabited	Uninhabited
Shirviyeh	Unknown: Probably southeast edge	Dar-e-Kavar (Dar-e-Fasa)	Gachpazan Soktoviyeh (A village just outside Fasa Gate)
Bagh-e-Now	East and Southeast parts of city	Bagh-e-Qotlogh	Khargahtarashan Bagh-e-Now Khaddash, Imana-bad, Sangi, Sanbak, Zendan (Rendan?), Seh-Shanbeh
Mosalla	Outside Northern City Wall	n/a	n/a
Jame' Atiq	City Center	Sarrajan (Palangeran) Part of Dashtak Dar al-Shafa	Kucheh-ye-Barmakan

Sources: *Shadd al-Izar; Farsnameh-ye-Naseri; Hezar-Mazar; Shiraznameh; Kotbi; Nozhat al-Qolub; Tarikh-e-Vassaf.*

19th Century Quarters and Population	Extant (1972) Graves and Landmarks	Remarks
Darb-e-Shahzadeh Meidan Shah ca. 12,000	Sheikh-e-Kabir (d. 982) Hassan Kiya (d. ca. 1203) Badal Family (14th century)	
Sang-e-Siyah Sar-e-Bagh Darb-e-Masjed Part of Sar-e-Dozak Ca. 10,500	Sibuyeh Nahvi (d. 796), Bibi Dokhtaran (14th cent.), Shah Manzar (date unknown) Masjed Now (ca. 1215)	*Bibi Dokhtaran* built near Beiza Gate
Uninhabited	See above, chpt. 1	Opposite Salm Gate
Part of Bala-Keft	Abesh Khatun (d. 1286)	Included areas both inside and outside city walls
Bala Keft Ca. 7,500	Hosein b. Musa (d. ca. 815) Ruzbehan Baqli (d. 1209) Sheikh Abu Zare' Ardebili (d. 1004)	Grave of Ruzbehan Family in area now called *Dar-e-Sheikh*
n/a	See chpts. 3, 6	Originally an area of gardens, dervish retreats, and cemetaries. Inhabited in since 1920s.
Bazar-e-Morgh Sar-e-Dozak, Lab-e-Ab Part of Eshaq Beg Sar-e-Bagh Ca. 20,000	Favorite burial place of Shirazi Seyyeds. For details, see chapter 6.	*Dashtak* is early name for *Dozak,* which was divided between *Sar-e-Dozak* and *Lab-e-Ab* in the 18th Century

Mosques

Mostowfi records that in 1340 Shiraz contained more than five hundred mosques, dervish retreats (*khaneqahs*), seminaries, and other pious foundations of the rich. Of the mosques, the sources have preserved the names of thirteen; three of these, the great congregational mosques *(masjed-e-jame'),* were the leading mosques of Shiraz in the fourteenth century. Although no trace remains of the great *Masjed-e-Jame'-e-Songhoriyeh,* two of the three have survived: the ninth-century *Masjed-e-Jame'-ye-Atiq* (Old Congregational Mosque—called simply *Jame' Atiq*) founded by the Saffarid Amru Leith, and the early thirteenth-century *Masjed-e-Jame'-ye-Now* (New Congregational Mosque) founded by the Salghurid Atabek Sa'd b. Zangi.[18]

Although in 1972 the Old Congregational Mosque was in poor condition, in Hafez's time it was considered among the most beautiful mosques in the world. On Thursdays, Fridays, and Saturdays, as many as two thousand women would assemble there to hear sermons. The *pishnamaz* or *imam* (prayer leader), the *khatib* (reader of the Friday sermon), and the *va'ez* (preacher) of this mosque were all important figures in the city.[19] Joneid Shirazi, poet and author of *Shadd al-Izar,* referred to his own post as preacher in this mosque as follows:

دو منصبند که با یک دگر نیا ید راست   مقام عاشق و وعظ پیشگاه عتیق

Two callings that clash with each other always
Are those of sufi lover and preacher in the Atiq.

The other surviving congregational mosque of Shiraz is the Masjed-e-Jame'-ye-Now, located in the Bahaliyeh area of the city about four hundred meters west of the Jame' Atiq. In 1972 this mosque, called simply Masjed-e-Now (New Mosque), survived in very ruined condition. It reached its zenith in the thirteenth century, when its *khatib* (reader of the Friday sermon) was the chief judge of Fars, Saraj al-Din Mokarram Fali (d. 1223). At that time its preachers included such notables as Sheikh Taj al-Din Ahmad Horr (d. thirteenth century), Sheikh Baha al-Din Mosalahi Beizavi (d. 1275), and Sheikh Sa'd al-Din Baghnovi (d. 1271).[20] During Hafez's lifetime, a century later, it was less important than the other two great mosques.

In addition to the great congregational mosques, Hafez's Shiraz contained numerous smaller mosques, which have all long disappeared. The founding inscription of one, dated 787/1385, was found in 1972 near the Rabat-e-Abesh. Many of these survive only as names in the sources. Table 4.2 (pp. 60–61) summarizes information in the sources concerning the founding, location, and preachers of the mosques of Shiraz in the fourteenth century. Some of these mosques carried the names of their endowers. Others might be associated with a family whose members were hereditary preachers of a certain mosque and were buried in its precincts. Still others were associated with a city neighborhood or with the inhabitants of another town who preferred to worship together in Shiraz.

Seminaries

Shiraz had dozens of seminaries (*madraseh,* pl. *madares*) in the fourteenth century, but none from that period has survived (see table 4.3, pp. 62–64). Today the oldest surviving seminary in the city is the Madraseh-ye-Mansouriyeh in the Dashtak district, founded in 1477 by Amir Seyyed Sadr al-Din Mohammad Dashtaki-Shirazi. He donated over ten thousand square meters of land for construction and endowed the school extensively, including as part of the endowment the village of Sokhtoviyeh, located just outside the Fasa gate.[21]

In Hafez's Shiraz, almost every pious person who could afford it would endow a seminary. These structures ranged from a few modest rooms to impressive buildings—if the Mansouriyeh indicates what existed a century earlier. That well-endowed school was strongly built of brick and plaster and had a hundred rooms for students on two stories and four main arches, each about sixteen meters high.

Table 4.3 summarizes information about the seminaries of Shiraz—their locations, founders, and famous teachers. Most of the founders were wealthy rulers, princesses, ministers, or chief judges, and their seminaries must have had both large physical plants and extensive endowments to pay for upkeep, teachers, students' stipends, and the very expensive handwritten books. Important figures were often buried in the seminaries, which became centers for pilgrimage as well as scholarship. Among the most important of the seminaries in Hafez's day were the Khatuniyeh, founded in 1343 by Tashi Khatun, mother of Shah Abu Eshaq Inju; the Mas'udiyeh, founded by Mas'ud Shah Inju; the Majdiyeh, founded by Qazi Majd al-Din Esma'il

Table 4.2. Mosques of Shiraz

Mosque & Sources	Location	Foundation	Remarks
Jame'Atiq (SA *passim*, SN 67)	City Center	Amru Leith Saffari 281/894	Most famous mosque of Shiraz. Many famous preachers, including the Baghnovi family. *Dar al-Mashaf* with inscription built by Shah Sheikh Abu Eshaq Inju in 752/1351. Mosque survives in poor condition.
Jame'-ye-Now (SA *passim*, SN 77)	*Bahaliyeh* District. Opposite tomb of Ahmad b. Musa	Atabek Sa'd b. Zangi ca. 613/1215	Largest mosque of Shiraz. Very important in 13th century (see chpt. 4). Survives in ruined condition.
Jame-ye-Songhoriyeh (NQ 138, SA 233)	Bagh-e-Now District, *Khargahtarashan* (Tent-makers) quarter.	Atabek Songhor b. Mowdud (1148–62)	Very important mosque in the 14th century. For preachers, see text. Part of Songhoriyeh complex, which included school and tombs. No trace remains.
Haj Ali *Assar* (HM 121)	Near bazaar of Bagh-e-Now	Haji Ali *Assar* (d. 1355)	Built near the tomb of Sheikh Mohammad *Baqqal* (d. 1269)
Sheikh Amin al-Din (Narak) (SA 256)	Bagh-e-Now District	Amin al-Din (?)	Build near the tomb of Shikh Mo'ayyed al-Din (d. 13th century)
Baghdadi (SA 129, 317, SN 184)	Unknown	Unknown	Preachers inclued: Ahmad Zarkub (d. 1387); *Pishnamaz* (prayer leader) Jamal al-Din Mohammad Kasa'i (d. 1272) and his son Zein al-Din (d. 1312).

Mosque & Sources	Location	Foundation	Remarks
Bagh-e-Now (SA *passim*)	Bagh-e-Now District	Baghnovi Family 7th/13th Century	Preached in by Baghnovi Family, including Sadr al-Din Mozaffar (d. 1289) and his sons Rokn al-Din Mansur *Rastgu* (d. 1332) and Zia al-Din (d. 1342)
Bahaliyeh (SA 88, SN 135)	Bahaliyeh District near Kazeroun Gate	Unknown	Preached in by Sheikh Mohammad Moqarezi (d. 1021)
Fakhri (SA 284)	Unknown	Fakhr al-Din Malek b. Malek al-Islam Tibi (ca. 1300)	Pishnamaz of this mosque was Imam Zahir al-Din *Khatib* (d. 14th century)
Jenazat (SA 119, 145)	Uncertain: either in Dar al-Salm area or in Bahaliyeh near the Kazeroun Gate	Unknown	Contained tombs of Faqih Sams al-Din Mohammad (d. 1368) and Ostad Fakhr al-Din (d. 1332)
Khasseh (SA 106)	Bahaliyeh District	Unknown	Mosque associated with Khajeh Ahmad Khasseh (d. 14th century). Preached in by Najm al-Din Kazerouni (d. after 1349)
Mas'udiyeh (SA 128)	Unknown	Mas'ud Shah Inju (d. 1342)	Preached in by Amir Seif al-Din Yousef *Va'ez* (d. 1362)
Yahya (SA 149, SN 169)	Salm Gate area	Sa'd al-Din Yahya Salehani	
Unknown	Adjoining Abesh Khatun	Hosein Esma'il (NFI) 787/1385	Inscription discovered by author in 1970. See photograph, figure 5.

Abbreviations: SA: *Shadd al-Izar;* SN: *Shiraznameh;* HM: *Hezar Mazar;* NQ: *Nozhat al-Qolub* (Persian text)

Table 4.3. Seminaries of Hafez's Shiraz

Sem. and Sources	Location	Foundation	Remarks
Aminiyeh (SA 356, 427; SN 78)	Darb-e-Estakhr District	Amid al-Din Asad Afzari (d. 1227) Minister of Atabek Sa'd	Teachers included Saraj al-Din Mokarram Fali (d. 1332) and Qazi Jamal al-Din Mesri (d. 1252)
Amini (SA 351, 408; SN 74)	Adjoining Jame' Atiq	Amin al-Din Banjir Kazerouni (12th century) Minister of Atabek Tekleh b. Zangi (1175–94)	Tomb of founder in the school. Teachers included Sheikh Abu Moslem Kazerouni (d. 1229)
Azodiyeh (SA 273–4, 362)	Bagh-e-Now District	Tarkan Khatun, widow of Atabek Sa'd b. Abu Bakr (d. 1260)	Named for founder's son, Azod al-Din Mohammad (d. 1263), who is buried next to school. Teachers included Qazi Baha al-Din Osman (d. 1380) and Sadr al-Din Mohammad Jowhari (d. 1368)
Banjir Khowzi (SA 296, 299, 535; SN 183)	Jame' Atiq District	Sheikh Banjir Khowzi (d. 1178)	Contained tomb of Sharaf al-Din b. Omar b. Zeki Bushkani (d. 1278)
Dar al-Shafa (FNN II, 134)	Jame' Atiq District	Shah Shoja' Mozaffari (14th century)	Seyyed Sharif Jorjani *Alameh* (d. 1413) appointed teacher here in 1377. His tomb is in this area.
Dashtaki (SA 321)	Dashtak District	Amir Seyyed Sadr al-Din Mohammad (d. 1363)	Adjoined Dashtaki family tombs. Perhaps later expanded into Mansuriyeh School.
Fakhriyeh (SA 416)	Unknown	Unknown	Teachers included Mowlana Nezam al-Din Esma'il Khorasani (d. ca. 1222)
Fazariyeh or Afzariyeh (FN 135ff; SA 262, 360–1, 397, 451)	Jame' Atiq District	Uncertain: Either in 10th or 11th century by Qazi Abu Taher Mohammad Sharaf Afzari (d. 1098)	Contained tomb of founder. Teachers included Qazi Baha al-Din Osman (d. 1380), Ekhtiyar al-Din Loqman Semnani (d. 14th century) and Mowlana Qazi al-Din Ayyub (d. ca. 1359)
Jamal al-Din Mesri (SA 357, SN 171)	Jame' Atiq District next to Fazariyeh School in *Givehduzan* Bazaar	Qazi Jamal al-Din Mesri (d. 1255), Chief Judge of Fars	Contained tomb of founder

Sem. and Sources	Location	Foundation	Remarks
Kermanshahiyeh (SA 399)	Unknown	Unknown	Teachers included Sheikh Shahab al-Din Ahmad Kermani (d. 1244)
Khatuniyeh (SA 290–2; SN 198)	Masjed Atiq District next to tomb of Ahmad b. Musa	Tashi Khatun (d. 1343), mother of Abu Eshaq Inju	Founder buried here
Korduchin TJY, 71	Unknown	Uncertain: Perhaps in 13th century by daughter of ruler of Kerman	Might have been built in 14th century by Korduchin, daughter of Abesh Khatun
Lala (NT 86; SA 447; SN 65)	Darb-e-Estakhr District	Abu Nasr Lala— served Atabek Manku Bars (1132–45)	Teachers included Sheikh Jamal al-Din Mohammad Neirizi (d. 12th century). Still important school in 14th century
Majd al-Din Rumi (SN 98)	Jame' Atiq District, *Sarrajan* Quarter	Majd al-Din Asad Rumi, ruler of Shiraz 1287–89	
Majdiyeh (IB 195)	Unknown	Qazi Majd al-Din Esma'il Fali (1272–1355), Chief Judge of Fars	Founder lived, worked, and received visitors in this school
Manku-Barsiyeh (NT 86; SN 65, 203)	Shirviyeh area	Atabek Manku Bars (1132–45)	Famous scholars buried here, including *hadith* scholar Heidar b. Monavvar (d. 1213)
Mas'udiyeh (SA 317; MTM 172–3)	Unknown	Mas'ud Shah Inju (d. 1342)	Teachers included Mo'in al-Din Ahmad Zarkub (d. 1387), author of *Shiraznameh*
Moqarreb (SA 239–40, 295; SN 84, 182)	Jame' Atiq District in the main bazaar	Amir Moqarreb al-Din Mas'ud, minister of Atabek Abu Bakr b. Sa'd (13th century)	Buildings still standing in 1320. Tomb of Qazi Imam al-Din Omar Beiza'I (d. 1276) on North side of school.
Moshrafiyeh (SA 212)	Unknown	Faqih Moshraf al-Din (d. 13th Century)	
Mosavi (SA 171)	Unknown	Seyyed Ezz al-Din Ahmad b. Ja'far Hoseini Mosavi *Naqib*	

continued

Table 4.3 (cont.)

Sem. and Sources	Location	Foundation	Remarks
Nasiriyeh (SA 266)	Bagh-e-Now District	Unknown	Sheikh Afzal al-Din Heras (d. ca. 1184) buried behind this school
Qarajeh (NT 86; SN 64–5)	Masjed Atiq District next to Fazariyeh School	Atabek Qarajeh, ruler of Shiraz ca. 1131	Still important school in the 14th century
Qavamiyeh (Hasan Kiya) (SA 379)	Near grave of Hasan Kiya in the Darb-e-Estakhr District	Haj Qavam al-Din Hasan, (d. 1352) minister of Abu Eshaq Inju	Teachers included Mowlana Sadr al-Din Mohammad Jowhari (d. 1368)
Razaviyeh (SA 323)	Unknown	Unknown	Teachers included Sharaf al-Din Ebrahim Dashtaki (d. 1386)
Samiyeh (SA 213–14)	Shirviyeh Area	Unknown	Contained tombs of Qazi Zein al-Din Ali Khonji (d. 1307) and his son Majd al-Din Esma'il (d. 1343)
Shahi (SA 253; TV 223–27)	Unknown	Khatun Korduchin, daughter of Abesh Khatun (14th century)	
Sharifi (SN 203	Masjed Atiq area, *Givehduzan* Bazaar	Uncertain: Perhaps 12th century	Contained tomb of probable founder, Seyyed Sharif Nezam al-Din Ahmad Alavi *Naqib* (d. 1136)
Songhoriyeh (SA *passim*)	Bagh-e-Now area, *Khargah-tarrashan* quarter	Atabek Songhor b. Mowdud (mid 12th century)	Founder buried here. School still existed in the 14th century as part of the *Songhoriyeh* complex
Taji (NT 86)	Unknown	Taj al-Din Shirazi, minister of Atabek Bozabeh (d. 1146)	
Zahedeh Khatun (SA 281–2; SN 67)	Bagh-e-Now area, next to tomb of Atabek Bozabeh	Zahedeh Khatun, widow of Atabek Bozabeh (d. 1147)	First administered by Hanafis; then by Shafi'is. Teachers included Sheikh Abu al-Fazl Neirizi (d. 1223)

Abbreviations: SA=*Shadd al-Izar.* SN=*Shiraznameh.* NT=*Nezam al-Tavarikh.* TV=*Tarikh-e-Vassaf.* FNN=*Farsnameh-ye-Naseri.* FN=*Farsnameh-ye-Ibn Balkhi.* TJY=*Tarikh-e-Jadid-e-Yazd.* MTM=*Montakhab-e-Tavarikh-e-Mo'ini.* IB: Ibn Battuta.

Fali (1272–1355), the chief judge of Fars under the Inju; Dar al-Shafa, founded by Shah Shoja Mozaffari, where Seyyed Sharif Jorjani Alameh came to teach in 1377; and Amidiyeh, founded in the thirteenth century by Khwajeh Amid al-Din Afzari, the minister of Atabek Sa'd b. Zangi.[22]

Other Buildings

In addition to mosques and seminaries, fourteenth-century Shiraz had other important buildings. The sources frequently refer to *rabats* and *khaneqahs* built around the teaching and living quarters of a famous holy person. After his death, the tomb would become a place of pilgrimage, a center for dervishes and teachers, and a burial place for disciples and members of his or her family.[23]

A *rabat* could also be a school. In Hafez's time, the renowned scholar of *hadith* (prophetic tradition) Sa'id al-Din Baliyani Kazeruni (d. 1357) taught at the Rabat-e-Khafif, originally built at the tomb of Sheikh-e-Kabir by Atabek Zangi in the second half of the twelfth century. By the fourteenth century, *rabat* had two meanings in Shiraz: in a limited sense, it was a retreat for sufis (in which sense it could also be called *khaneqah*); in a broader meaning, it was a complex of buildings centered around the tomb of a holy person.[24]

Bazaars

When Ibn Battuta first visited Shiraz in 1327, he noted that the main bazaar of Shiraz extended as far as the north door of the Old Congregational Mosque. He praised the entire bazaar for its beauty and good order, especially the fruit market, which was just outside the great mosque. According to his account, each guild operated in a separate area of the bazaar and there was no mixing of the shops. The sources also mention smaller bazaars— the Khuzestan and Givehduzan (sandalmakers')—in the area of the Jame' Atiq, which may have been sections of the main bazaar. There were also smaller, neighborhood bazaars, such as the Bazar-e-Bagh-e-Now.[25]

Hospitals

In the tenth century, the Buyid ruler Azod al-Dowleh had endowed a large hospital (Dar al-Shafa) in Shiraz, but that building fell into ruins during the anarchy of the late Buyid and early Seljuq periods. In the thirteenth century, Atabek Abu Bakr and his minister Moqarreb al-Din Mas'ud endowed another hospital in the Salm Gate area (located near the *Dar al-Salm* Cemetery).

By the beginning of the fourteenth century, this hospital's endowment had been looted and its buildings had fallen into disrepair. At that time the Il-Khan's famous minister, Rashid al-Din, appointed the Shirazi physician Najm al-Din Mahmud b. Elyas director of the hospital and executor of its endowment. Rashid al-Din also added the income from two hundred jaribs of grain land, animals, cloth, skins, and 10,000 dinars in cash to the hospital's yearly stipend, and instructed his deputies and officials to pay this stipend regularly every year without requiring a new written order.[26]

THE ECONOMY: CITY OF ROSES AND TAXES

Supporting hundreds of mosques, seminaries, and other foundations in a city with an estimated population of fifty or sixty thousand, which itself produced very little, put a heavy burden on the economy of Fars. Although Shiraz owed some of its prosperity to its position on the trade route between the Persian Gulf ports and the important cities of northern Iran, the town's real economic bases were the agriculture of Fars and its status as a center of government and administration.

Throughout its history, Shiraz's prosperity had depended on its being a center of government for southern Iran. The existence of a major political center at Shiraz has meant that much of the revenue collected in Fars stayed in the province instead of supporting courts and governors in other areas. The economic stagnation in Shiraz during the nineteenth century happened when the city lost her political importance, in this case to the northern cities of Tabriz and Teheran. In the fourteenth century, political decline also brought economic disaster when it meant that an area's productivity benefited only a distant capital.[27]

Agriculture, Food, and Industry

The agriculture of Fars served two functions: first, to feed Shiraz and the other cities of the province; second, to produce crops for export to other parts of Iran. Cereal grains, chiefly wheat and barley, were the most important crops of Fars and provided Shiraz with its supply of bread. Farms around the city on the Shiraz plain produced most of Shiraz's food, since long-distance transportation would both be expensive and cause spoilage of many kinds of produce.

Shirazi cuisine in the fourteenth century, as recorded in the verses of the poet of food, Sheikh At'ameh, was both varied and nutritious, although heavy for modern tastes. The recipes in the sheikh's poems reflect the availability of a variety of foodstuffs from well-developed truck farming near the city. Some of the Shirazi specialties he describes are:

maqilba: A porridge (*ash*) made of meat, animal fat, meatballs, sheep intestine, wheat, beans, flat beans, beets, onions, turnips, carrots, cabbage, and leeks. Connoisseurs ate this concoction for the taste of the sheep intestine, which they considered a delicacy.

mokhla: Fried eggplant chopped up with fatty browned meat, served with lime juice and bread.

sokhtu: Sheep intestine stuffed with rice, saffron, onions, peas, hot spices, meat or liver, and fat.

zonaj: The same thing covered with saffron and fried in animal fat.[28]

Nutritionally, it would be hard to improve on these foods. In addition to these dishes, based on vegetables, mutton, sheep organs, and animal fat, the poet describes how the Shirazis consumed fresh fruits (especially grapes and melons), cheese, and sweets made from sugar, honey, nuts, and dates.[29]

The most important export crops of the Shiraz region were processed grapes and flower essences. In the fourteenth century Shiraz produced a kind of grape called *mesqali,* considered of excellent quality. In addition to their value as fresh fruit, grapes were also processed into wine, vinegar, molasses, raisins, and *qureh* (small, sour grapes used in cooking). Rashid al-Din was especially interested in expanding vineyard cultivation, and gave it careful attention on his private estates near Shiraz.

Since the first centuries of Islam, Fars, particularly in the warm lowlands, had been a center of cultivation of flowers and extraction of flower essences *(araq, rowghan)* for perfumes and medicines. In the tenth century, Fars produced some of the best aromatic herbs and perfumes in the world.

In the fourteenth century, violet, jasmine, and narcissus grew at Bishapur near Kazeroun, and, according to Mostowfi, "the rose water made [in Firuz-abad] has a finer perfume and is superior to that of all other lands."[30] Rashid al-Din supplied his hospitals from the medicinal essences of Fars. In a letter to an agent in Shiraz, he placed an order for the following oils: 100 *man* (ca. 300 kilograms) of violet oil; 20 *man* of jasmine oil; 50 *man* of almond blossom oil; 300 man of sweetbriar *(nastaran)* oil; 20 *man* of narcissus oil.

Textile production, including the weaving of cotton grown near the city, was the major industry of Shiraz. Kazeroun, ninety miles west of Shiraz, had been one of the greatest producers of linen *(katan)* in the world, but by the fourteenth century cotton had almost entirely replaced linen in the textile industry. During this period Kazeroun was still famous for her textiles, but produced mostly muslin (from cotton) and only a small amount of linen. According to the *Nozhat al-Qolub,* the regions of Shiraz, Abarqu, Kazeroun, Lar, and Darabgerd all grew cotton. Early in the fifteenth century, Shiraz was weaving and exporting cloth woven of cotton and silk, including crepe and taffeta.

Except for the textile weavers, the industries of Shiraz worked for local consumption. The city's position as the capital of a local dynasty for much of the fourteenth century was a great stimulus to her local industry, with the ruler, his court, and his armies creating a demand for goods and services. A city the size and importance of Shiraz had the numerous trades and crafts necessary to supply both itself and the surrounding rural areas. With the close connection between Shiraz and the surrounding countryside, most urban trades were related to agriculture—produce dealing, food processing, and the like. Among the trades named in the sources were *assar* (oil presser), *akkar* (gardener), *allaf* (forage dealer), *tonakaki* and *khabbaz* (baker), *qannad* (pastry and candy maker), *dorudgar* (carpenter), *sarraj* or *palangar* (saddle maker), *givehduz* (sandal maker), *hallaj* (cotton beater), *gachpaz* (plaster maker), *dabbagh* (tanner), *baqqal* (grocer)—and *shattar* (hired hoodlum).

Revenue and Taxation

Since the Abbasid and Buyid periods, Fars had experienced a long-term decline in revenue, occasionally checked by the reforms of a strong ruler. In the year 815 the Abbasid Caliph Ma'mum set the total taxes for Fars (including Kerman and the Persian Gulf coast) at about 6.07 million dinars. A century later, Ali b. Isa, the minister of the Caliph al-Muqtadir, set the total taxes for Fars, Kerman, and ships' duties at the port of Siraf at 5.44 million dinars. Fars achieved its greatest prosperity and produced the most revenue under the Buyid ruler Azod al-Dowleh in the tenth century. His treasury collected a total of 7.828 million dinars from Fars, Kerman, and Oman, as shown in table 4.4.[31]

Table 4.4. Revenue Under the Buyids

District	Revenue in Millions of Dinars
Fars (including Siraf and ships' duties)	5.040
Shiraz district, including Gerd-e-Fana Khosrow	0.735
Kerman	1.750
Oman (including Iranian Baluchestan)	0.303
Total	7.828

The devastation of the Seljuq period in the eleventh and twelfth centuries reduced revenues to about 2.34 million dinars. There are no revenue figures for the Salghurid period, but relative political stability and some economic recovery must have brought an increase, although not to pre-Seljuq levels. In the Mongol period, the disruption caused by invasions, the raids by enemies of the Il-Khans such as the Chaghatai and Nikudaris (see chapter 2), the conversion of agricultural land to pasture for nomads, and the ruinous tax policies of the early Il-Khans all brought a sharp decline in both productivity and revenue. For example, the region of Kerbal in the Marvdasht plain, which had produced 700,000 *kharvars* (about 2,200 metric tons) of grain during the reign of Azod al-Dowleh, produced only 300,000 *kharvars* under the Salghurid Atabek Sa'd b. Abu Bakr in 1260. By the late thirteenth century, before the reforms of Ghazan Khan, the area's maximum output was 175,000 *kharvars*, which yielded 42,000 *kharvars* in taxes.[32]

The reforms of Ghazan Khan (r. 1295–1303) and his minister Rashid al-Din brought a temporary improvement in the economic situation and an increase in revenue. At the beginning of Ghazan Khan's reign, the total revenue of Iran, excluding Khorasan, was 17 million dinars. The Ghazanid reforms raised that figure to 21 million, but by 1339, according to

Mostowfi, "because of renewed anarchy, the revenue probably does not amount to half this sum."[33]

In the fourteenth century, Fars by default was one of the wealthiest provinces of the Il-Khanid state, with a yearly income of 2.87 million dinars. In the pre-Mongol era both Azarbaijan and Eraq-e-Ajam (Esfahan and West Central Iran) had been wealthier areas, but the Mongol invasions of the thirteenth century had reduced the revenue of these two regions to 2.35 and 2.16 million dinars, respectively. At that time, the Shiraz district itself had eclipsed Esfahan: in 1339 the revenue from the Shiraz region was 450,000 dinars, while that of Esfahan was only 350,000.[34]

From the middle of the eleventh century, the individual tax burden rose as the total revenues collected from Fars declined. During the thirteenth and fourteenth centuries the Mongol military aristocrats—and the Iranian civil officials who served them, themselves exempt from many kinds of taxes—collected taxes and rents from their own peasantry and built enormous private fortunes and estates. Much of the endowment of the numerous seminaries, mosques, and other foundations in Shiraz described in the preceding section came from the holdings of these landowners. At the same time, the tax burden on the peasants forced them to flee the countryside and abandon their arable land. The consequent loss of revenue meant more pressure of taxation on those who remained on the land.[35]

The Il-Khan minister Rashid al-Din noted these specific abuses in the taxation system in the later thirteenth and early fourteenth century: arbitrary assessment and collection of taxes several times a year, often in advance; frequent extraordinary levies (nemari, taklifat); drafts (barat) frequently written on the revenues of a rural area; and the absence of public security.[36] Attempting to eliminate this uncontrolled looting of the country's wealth, Ghazan Khan pointed out to his commanders that their oppression of the peasant was to their own disadvantage. He told them:

> I am not taking the side of the Tajik [Persian] peasant. If it were the best policy to loot them all, then there is no one in a better position than I to say, "Let us loot them together." However, if afterwards you expect food and supplies from me, I will abuse you. You must consider, when you oppress the peasant and take his animals, seed, and grain, what you are going to receive from me in the future.[37]

TAX INSCRIPTION, 15TH CENTURY

In Fars the number and kinds of taxes began multiplying in the second quarter of the thirteenth century, during the reign of Atabek Abu
Bakr b. Sa'd and before the rule of the Il-Khans in Fars. Needing money
for tribute to the Mongols, for his wives, and for the upkeep of his armies,
the Atabek revoked many titles of *eqta'* (military fief) land in the *garmsir*

and imposed new taxes. In Shiraz he taxed entering goods, houses, and water. He also taxed animals and food (except wheat and barley), and private lands at a portion of the *divan* (state land) rate.

During and after the Il–Khanid period, Iran experienced a taxation explosion. The Soviet historian Petrushevsky lists forty-seven kinds of taxes collected during the Mongol period in addition to the basic land tax (*kharaj*).[38] The most important tax for the Shirazis was the *tamgha,* a tax collected on all city crafts and trades, from the richest merchant to the poorest peddler. An inscription (p. 71) dating from about 1450 names some of the taxes collected in the city, including a variety of *tamgha.*[39] The inscription mentions:

Taxes on marriages (*zan* [or *vazn*] *halali*) (or on weights and measures; the exact reading is unclear)

A tax on fruit *(rosum-e-miveh)*

A surtax on *tamgha (ezafeh ma'khuz-e-tamgha)*

Taxes on tanneries *(dabbaghkhaneh),* soap makers *(sabunkhaneh),* brothels *(beit al-lotf),* wine–shops *(sharabkhaneh),* opium dens *(banj-khaneh),* and gambling houses *(gomarkhaneh)*

Contractor's payments from the department of punishments (?) *(moqate'eh-ye-divan-e-siyasi)*

Road duties or tolls *(baj-e-rah)*

Tax for road protection *(rosum-e-rahdari)*

Tax on burial preparation *(rosum-e-ghassali)*

Tax on water of Zaijan Mountain taken for the fortress [of Fahandezh?]

CONCLUSION
Hafez's lyrics, and the works of his contemporaries, all emerged from a specific physical setting. Their backdrop was the history, geography, and

economy of Shiraz in the fourteenth century. Their achievements grew out of the rich urban life of Shiraz: the security from rampaging tribes and armies offered by its walls and gates; the neighborhoods and bazaars where Shirazis lived and worked; the communal prayers and sermons preached at the Old Congregational Mosque; the lessons and lectures at the Khatuniyeh Seminary; and the sufi gatherings at the Rabat-e-Khafif.

There existed another side to all this religiosity. For who could long endure the monotony of constant piety, fasts, and prayer? One aspect of city life already noted was the violence of besieging armies and uncontrollable city mobs. Still another side of life in Shiraz was hedonism and debauchery *(rendi)*, the disregard of conventional morality in pursuit of the pleasures of music, drink, sex, and drugs. This desire to ignore the dictates of both reason and religion is what Hafez evokes so beautifully in his poetry, and where he finds the most powerful response in his countrymen. For example:

پیران جاهل شیخان گمراه مارا به رندی افسانه کردند

وز فعل عابد استغفر الله از دست زاهد کردیم توبه

The ignorant sages, the deluded preachers
Have made me a legend among the *rend*.
We have repented of the ascetic,
And have said, "God forbid," to the deeds of the pious.

5

The City Administration

Everyone's teeth are dulled by sour foods
Except the judge's. His are dulled only by sweets.

—Sa'adi, Golestan

In Hafez's time, running Shiraz, a city of sixty thousand (sometimes unruly) inhabitants in the fourteenth century, meant keeping the population fed, quiet, and paying the taxes that supported the ruler's court and army. But if ruling Shiraz was simpler then than now, it still required the rulers to establish and preserve a delicate balance among themselves, their officers, and the numerous centers of influence in the city.

Above all, whoever ruled Shiraz needed enough stability to collect those taxes that paid tax collectors and soldiers. For many reasons, that stability never came easily to Shiraz. Its economy depended upon the surrounding countryside, and natural and man-made disasters were always threatening the city's fragile peace and well-being. At any time, floods, droughts, and invasions could bring famine and wipe out the city's economic base. For centuries, uprisings among the tribes of Fars had threatened the security of the towns and made roads unsafe for travel and trade. Inside the city walls, rebellions, riots, and factional strife among the Shirazis were a constant threat. Finally, outside the walls, external enemies—rival Mozaffarids, Chupanids, and Jalayerids—were always looking to take Shiraz by force or plot.[1]

THE RULING ELITE

In a famous poem known as "Rejal-e-Mamlekat-e-Fars," Hafez describes the city's power structure during the reign of Abu Eshaq. He names five persons—a ruler, a minister, two judges, and a sufi sheikh—who, in different ways, possessed great influence and power in fourteenth-century Shiraz.[2] The five were:

The Ruler: Shah Sheikh Abu Eshaq

The Advisor and Minister of the Ruler: Haji Qavam al-Din Tamghachi (d. 1352)[3]

The Chief Judge *(Qazi al-Qozat)* of Fars: Qazi Majd al-Din Esma'il Fali (1271–1355)

A Judge and Scholar: Qazi Azod al-Din Iji (d. 1355), who served Abu Eshaq and composed works on theology, ethics, and grammar[4]

A Leader of the Sufis: Sheikh Amin al-Din Baliyani Kazeruni (d. 1344), from a famous family of scholars, and known by his title of Sheikh al-Eslam[5]

The Ruler and His Court

In the seven hundred years from its founding until Hafez's time, a Shirazi had never ruled Shiraz. Nor, except for one century of Deilamite rule in the tenth and eleventh centuries, had Shiraz been subject to an Iranian ruler. From the Seljuq period in the eleventh century there arose in Iran the idea that only persons of Turkish background were destined to rule.[6] Events in Shiraz supported this stereotype. From the middle of the eleventh century the city's rulers were Seljuq *amirs* and *atabeks* (regents), Salghurid *atabeks* and *khatuns* (princesses), and Mongol officers.

Although the Inju and Mozaffarid rulers of Shiraz in the fourteenth century were not originally Turkish or Mongol, their families had intermarried with ruling Turkish and Mongol dynasties such as the Jalayerids of Baghdad and the Qarakhitai of Kerman. Through residence at the Mongol court, the local rulers had learned its practices. Family ties, imitation of Mongol court ceremony, and the presence of Turkish commanders in the Inju and Mozaffarid armed forces all gave a distinct Turkish-Mongol cast to the ruling house.[7]

The prominence of the women of the ruling house was more characteristic of nomadic Turkish and Mongol practice than of urban Persian customs. Ibn Battuta reports that when the women of Shiraz left their homes they completely covered their bodies and faces, but Tashi Khatun, mother of Abu Eshaq Inju, usually went out with her face uncovered, "as is the custom with Turkish women."[8] Among the Salghurids, the princesses Torkan, Abesh, and Korduchin either ruled Shiraz independently or acted as regent. In 1365 Khan Sultan, the daughter of Amir Keikhosrow b. Mahmud Shah Inju, took command of the defense of Shiraz against Shah Shoja during the absence of her husband (and Shah Shoja's brother) Shah Mahmud. According to the *Farsnameh-ye-Naseri*, "She took such care for the walls and towers that conquest of the city was impossible. Each day and night she inspected and encouraged the defenders, thus saving the city for Shah Mahmud."[9]

Modern (male) Iranian historians take a dark view of this period, and cite the "harmful influence of women" in the Il-Khanid court as contributing to the "general moral depravity of the age."[10] These historians love to retell the story of how the wife of Sheikh Hasan-e-Kuchek, fearing for herself and her lover, murdered her husband by squeezing his testicles.[11] Sheikh Hasan-e-Kuchek himself had forced his mother to sleep with an impostor posing as his father, Teimur Tash b. Amir Chupan. Abu Sa'id Bahador, the last ruling Il-Khan, was killed by his wife Baghdad Khatun in revenge for his affection for Delshad Khatun, a rival wife, and for his killing of her (Baghdad Khatun's) father (Amir Chupan) and her brothers.

The Minister

Although the ruler was the most powerful figure in Shiraz, he seldom chose to exercise direct control over the day-to-day affairs of the city. He left that work to appointed officials supervised by the *vazir* or minister, whose basic task was collecting revenue for the ruler. This meant supervising public order and trade through the police *(Shahneh, darugheh)*, tax collectors *(basqaq)*, and the regulator of weights and measures in the bazaar *(mohtaseb)*.[12]

In spite of his power, the *vazir* did not usually enjoy a secure tenure or a long life. Amir Zahir al-Din Ebrahim Sarrab, minister of Abu Eshaq, was killed by a *rend* (street ruffian) hired by his rivals in 1344 after only a few months in office. His rival and successor, Shams al-Din Sa'en Qazi Semnani, was killed in the following year while on an expedition against

the Mozaffarids of Kerman.[13] Abu Eshaq executed another of his ministers, Ghiyath al-Din Ali Yazdi, in 1345 following accusations of adultery
with the ruler's mother.[14]

The ministers of the Mozaffarids did not fare much better. Shah Shoja
had five ministers, most of whom met violent deaths. He had his first minister, Qavam al-Din Mohammad Saheb Ayyar, tortured and executed in
1363 after four years in office. The executioners cut up his body and sent
the pieces to the various cities of the Mozaffarid realm. Qavam al-Din
had been on very good terms with Hafez, who praised him in a number
of poems and who commemorated his death as follows:

اعظم قوام الدین دولت و دین آنکه بر درش   از بهر خاک بوس نمودی فلک سجود

با آن جلال و آن عظمت زیر خاک شد   در نصف ماه ذی قعده از عرصه وجود

تا کس امید جود ندارد دگر ز کس   آمد حروف سال وفاتش امید جود

The great Qavam al-Din, the one for whom
Heaven prostrated itself to kiss the dust of his door,
With all of his splendor and magnificence, has fallen to earth
In the middle of *Zu'l-qa'deh,* he has left this life.
So no longer should one hope for generosity from another.
The year of his death comes from the words "hope for
generosity."[15]

It could be equally dangerous for a minister to be in the favor of a ruler,
for a king's fall or death usually meant the fall of his favored minister.
Thus Borhan al-Din Fathollah, who had served Amir Mobarez al-Din
Mohammad b. Mozaffar for fourteen years, lost his life in 1358 when the
ruler's sons deposed and blinded their father.[16]

Two of the greatest ministers of this era managed long terms of office
and natural deaths. One was Khwajeh Qavam al-Din Hasan Tamghachi,
the minister of Abu Eshaq, who died in 1353 during the Mozaffarid siege
of Shiraz.[17] According to the sources, Qavam al-Din was a model vazir:
generous, loyal, cultured, and religious. He not only generously endowed
seminaries and other public works, but was also instrumental in estab-

lishing Abu Eshaq's circle of poetry and high living. He may have brought
the young Hafez into the group of Inju court poets who enjoyed Abu
Eshaq's patronage and who praised the young ruler in their verses. Qavam
al-Din had his own circle of learned men and poets, of which Hafez was
probably a member.[18]

Another minister who enjoyed a rare long term of office was Khwajeh Jalal al-Din Turanshah, the minister of Shah Shoja from 1369 until
that ruler's death in 1384. Turanshah rose to power for faithful service to
the ruler in adversity. In 1364, after Shah Shoja had surrendered Shiraz to
his brother Shah Mahmud and his Jalayerid allies, he withdrew toward
Kerman by way of Abarqu. Turanshah, who was governor in Abarqu, joined
Shah Shoja's retinue and provided as best he could for his forces. For the
next year Turanshah accompanied Shah Shoja in his difficult campaigns in
Kerman, where the prince had to rebuild an army to recapture Shiraz from
his brother. This loyalty to a patron in distress earned Turanshah the trust
and gratitude of the ruler, who appointed him minister in 1369 after Shah
Shoja had earlier imprisoned one minister and executed his successor.

Unlike the patrician Salghurid ministers, the origins of the ministers
of the Inju and Mozaffarid periods are obscure. But whatever his origins,
Khwajeh Turanshah, like Qavam al-Din Hasan, was a serious patron of
the arts and poetry. He donated a Qoran copied by the calligrapher Yahya
b. Jamal Sufi in 745–46/1344–45 to the Old Congregational Mosque.[19]
He was also a patron of Hafez, who praised him in many of his odes and
lyrics, sometimes by name and sometimes by such titles as Asef-e-Sani
(the second Asef), Asef-e-Dowran (the Asef of the age), and Khwajeh-
ye-Jahan (nobleman of the world).[20] Khwajeh Turanshah died in 1385,
six months after the death of Shah Shoja. Hafez commemorated the minister's death in these verses:

آصف عهد زمان جان جهان تورانشاه   که در این مزرعه جز دانه خیرات نکشت

ناف هفته بدواز ماه صفر کاف و الف   که بگلشن شد و این گلخن پردود بهشت

آنکه میلش سوی حق بینی و حق گوئی بود   سال تاریخ وفاتش طلب از میل بهشت

Turanshah, the Asef of the age, the spirit of the world,
Who planted nothing but the seeds of charity on this earth,

Rose to paradise and the stove of heaven
In the middle of the week, on the twenty-first of Safar.
Whoever desires truth and righteousness,
Seek the year of his death from the words "in search of heaven"
[میل بهشت = 787/1385].

The Judges (Qazis): The Shirazi Top Drawer

In fourteenth-century Shiraz the king and his minister were outsiders. Their first task was ruling a larger kingdom and they dealt directly only with those matters in Shiraz that affected security in their greater realm. Yet Shiraz was vital to the ruler. It represented both a secure capital and a source of revenue to support his court and army. At first glance, this attitude of the Injus and Mozaffarids toward Shiraz might not seem especially pro-urban, but their view was a clear change from the Mongol policy of contempt for and deliberate ruin of the cities. During the lifetime of Hafez, Shiraz witnessed a return, albeit on a small scale, to the attitudes of the earlier Buyid and Seljuq periods when rulers had actively encouraged urban life and development.[21]

By establishing an urban, as opposed to a nomadic, capital in the late Il-Khanid period, the Mongol rulers began to identify their own interests, at least to some extent, with those of the city. If the capital was to reflect a ruler's power, it needed suitable public buildings and a cultural life with learned men to teach in its schools and poets to sing the praises of the prince and his ministers. If it was to pay taxes and provide a secure military base, it had to be run in an orderly fashion with the cooperation of at least some of its influential citizens. Inju and Mozaffarid princes and ministers, both by choice and necessity, left most of the administration of Shiraz to the city's influential inhabitants. But the city was not independent or autonomous in any real sense. The ruler's power, when he chose to exercise it, was almost unlimited, and he would occasionally use his position to intervene directly in city affairs, removing one local official and replacing him with another.[22]

From Ra'is to Qazi

The ruler and his *vazir* needed a loyal official in Shiraz with a local power base. In the Buyid period this person had been the *ra'is*, but by the fourteenth century the title *ra'is* in Shiraz denoted only a *kalu*, or neighborhood chief.[23] In Shiraz, during the Buyid period, the family of *Mard-âsâ* held this title.[24] In the early eleventh century, one of the daughters of this family married the chief judge *(qazi al-qozat)* of Fars, Qazi Abu Nasr b. Abu Mohammad Abdollah Afzari. The next Afzari, Qazi Abdollah b. Abu Nasr, inherited both the chief judgeship from his father's family and the *riyasat* from his mother's. The author of the *Farsnahemh-ye-Ibn Balkhi* adds, "this Abdollah was the ancestor of the present [ca. 1106] qazi al-qozat, and from that time the chief judgeship and the *riyasat* of Fars has been in this family, both by right of inheritance and by merit."[25]

By the thirteenth century, the *ra'is* had lost his importance in Shiraz and the chief judge, *qazi al-qozat,* had become the most important and powerful local official serving under the ruler and his minister.[26] The judge was the authority on religious law, and as such had jurisdiction over the many activities covered by that law—property, commerce, religious practice, family, inheritance, and some parts of criminal law. Since the law governing the Islamic community was the law of God, the person interpreting and applying it held power in both civil and religious affairs. In addition to the chief judge of Fars there were other, subordinate judges in the city who made up the "judicial branch" of the government.

Judges and Rulers

The chief judge was a key member of the ruling establishment. He acted in the ruler's name, and the ruler appointed him and could theoretically dismiss him at will. The chief judge, however, also represented the inhabitants of the city in their dealings with the government. There are numerous examples of the *qazi's* acting on behalf of the Shirazis as well as on behalf of the ruler. In the thirteenth century Atabek Abu Bakr appointed Majd al-Din Esma'il Fali (d. 1268) chief judge with the express mission of reviewing old land titles and confiscating land his father, Atabek Sa'd b. Zangi, had given out in *eqta'* (feudal tax-farms). This judge's grandson, also named Majd al-Din Esma'il, inherited the chief judgeship and was one of Hafez's five nobles of Fars during the reign of Abu Eshaq. It was this Majd al-Din who averted looting and bloodshed in Shiraz by arranging for Amir Pir Hosein Chupani to enter the city peacefully in 1340 after the citizens had previously expelled him and his forces.[27]

The younger Qazi Esma'il was also part of a famous case of a chief judge's defying a ruler's orders on behalf of the Shirazis. As Ibn Battuta tells this story, in 1310 Sultan Oljaitu, who had embraced Shi'ism, ordered the Friday sermon *(khotbeh)* in the cities of Iraq and Iran to be read in the name of Ali, without including the names of the first three caliphs. This command met such violent opposition in Baghdad, Esfahan, and Shiraz that the *khatib,* fearing for his life, was unable to obey. Furious at this disobedience, the Sultan ordered the chief judges of the three cities to report to his camp in Azarbaijan. Qazi Esma'il, the chief judge of Fars, reached the Mongol camp first, where the Sultan ordered him thrown before his pack of man-eating dogs. The Qazi's faith, however, resulted in a miracle: the dogs sat quietly at his feet. The Sultan, convinced of Majd al-Din's holiness, gave him valuable gifts and cancelled his pro-Shia order.[28]

The chief judges were very much a part of the economic elite. Holding vast wealth in land, they shared much of the economic outlook of the Turkish and Mongol military aristocracy.[29] Chief judges made extensive endowments to seminaries and other pious foundations. Qazi Majd al-Din, following the miraculous escape described above, received a grant of one hundred villages in the region of Jamkan, about sixty miles south of Shiraz in one of the richest agricultural areas in Fars.[30] In addition to the income from their estates, the judges received direct stipends from the government. Both Qazi Majd al-Din Esma'il and Qazi Azod al-Din Iji received payments of cash, skins, and riding animals from Rashid al-Din, the great Il-Khanid minister.[31]

Although the satirist Obeid Zakani called the *qazi* "the one whom everyone curses," and described the *qazi*'s eyes as "bowls that are never filled," the chief judge of Fars enjoyed not only great power and wealth, but also enormous respect from even the ruler.[32] Rulers and ministers would entrust judges with important state missions, such as Qazi Azod al-Din's unsuccessful peace mission from Abu Eshaq to Amir Mohammad Mozaffar in 1353. Qazi Borhan al-Din Osman Kuhgiluye'i, chief judge under Shah Shoja from 1366 to 1380, acted as mediator between the imprisoned and blinded Amir Mohammad and his sons.[33] The ambassadors of Sultan Abu Sa'id and Shah Sheikh Abu Eshaq would sit before Qazi Majd al-Din holding their ears, a gesture of great honor and respect among the Mongols otherwise made only to kings. The nobles of the city would visit Qazi Esma'il every morning and evening; the ruler's wife and sister would bring their quarrels over inheritance for him to settle. The Shirazis did not call Majd al-Din simply Qazi, but addressed him as Mowlana 'A' zam (supreme master) and gave him this title in records and marriage licenses.[34]

Table 5.1 (pp. 84–85) summarizes the information in the sources concerning the chief judges of Fars. There are numerous gaps, especially for the sixth/twelfth century, and the chronology and order are not exact. In some cases it is not clear whether a judge was actually the Qazi al-Qozat or an important, but subordinate, judge. The information in the tables does reveal, though, that until the middle of the fourteenth century most chief judges of Shiraz were members of three important families originating in different parts of Fars: Fazari (or Afzari), Beiza'i, and Fali-Sirafi.[35] The exceptions to this rule were a few outsiders or were Alavis (seyyeds) who had married into the family of Fali-Sirafi.

Until the capture of Shiraz by the Mozaffarids in 1353, the office of chief judge was virtually hereditary within either the Beiza'i or some branch of the (conjoined) Fali/Afzari family. Amir Mohammad and Shah Shoja, the Mozaffarid rulers of Shiraz, may have appointed outsiders to the post in order to weaken the Fali-Sirafis, who had been closely associated with the Inju rulers.

The Fali-Sirafi family, whose genealogy is partially reconstructed in the appendix, far surpassed other Shirazi families of the town in both wealth and prestige. Its members did not marry into more modest families of scholars and preachers such as Baghnovi, Zarkub, Ruzbehan, and the like.[36] They intermarried only with families at the top of Shirazi society—ministers, other judges, and naqibs (chiefs of the Alavis). A change of dynasty and the death of the Fali-Sirafi patriarch, however, brought an end to this family's power. It lost the post of chief judge after the Mozaffarid capture of Shiraz in 1353 and the death of the second Majd al-Din Esma'il in 1355. After this setback, the family never recovered its influence.

The chief judge and the ruler maintained a delicate balance of power throughout the thirteenth and fourteenth centuries. In the second quarter of the thirteenth century, Atabek Abu Bakr, fearing the growing power and wealth of the seyyeds in the city, dismissed his chief judge, Seyyed Ezz al-Din Eshaq Alavi, the naqib of Shiraz. However, the ruler made no radical change in the office, since the new chief judge, although not a seyyed, was related to the previous one.[37] Later in the century, in 1279, Suqun-chaq No'in, the Mongol ruler of Shiraz, planned to appoint Naser al-Din Abdullah Beiza'i as chief judge of Fars. The governor gathered the judges, *seyyeds*, sheikhs, and other city notables to confirm his decision, but he met resistence from a group supporting Rokn al-Din Yahya Fali-Sirafi. Suqunchaq No'in would not act without unanimous support from the urban elite, so he arranged a compromise by which the two men would share the office.[38] Qazi Rokn al-Din, like his son Majd al-Din Esma'il, would occasionally resist the civil authorities and get away with it. Rokn al-Din bitterly opposed the Jewish governor of Shiraz, Shams al-Dowleh Malek-al-Yahud, who cultivated the favor of the religious classes and who claimed to be a secret Muslim. This opposition was reported to Sa'd al-Dowleh, the Il-Khan's Jewish minister, who took no action against the Qazi.[39]

Following the death of Qazi Majd al-Din Esma'il al-Din Esma'il in 1355, Amir Mohammad Mozaffar took the unusual step of combining the posts of chief judge and minister, appointing his *vazir* Borhan al-Din Fathollah to the post of *qazi al-gozat*. By combining the two offices, Amir Mohammad hoped to weaken the influence of the Fali-Sirafi family, which had been closely associated with the house of Inju.[40] As a newcomer to Shiraz and very determined to enforce strict religious orthodoxy, Amir Mohammad required a chief judge of proved loyalty. The new ruler trusted almost no one, however, and there were few candidates for the judgeship who possessed both the required learning and loyalty.

The chief judge of Fars occupied a powerful but delicate position between the rulers and the Shirazis. Theoretically, the ruler could dismiss and appoint chief judges at will; in reality he rarely did so. Theoretically, the chief judge could criticize the rulers for violations of religious law (which were frequent during this period); he rarely did so. The two depended on each other. The judge needed the ruler for the power to enforce his decisions; the ruler needed a judge who commanded (through his personality, learning, and family connections) enough of a following among the Shirazis to make his opinions effective and to ensure the smooth running of the city. If the judge chose his battles carefully, he could use his prestige and local support to take independent action against the ruler.

Poets of that era testify to the power and prestige of the chief judge of

Table 5.1. Chief Judges of Fars

Name	Dates	Remarks	Sources
I. Fazâri (Afzâri) Family			FN, 135–40 SA, 258–60 SN, 151
Qazi Abu Mohammad Abdullah Fazari	4th/10th Century	Chief Judge during reign of Azod al-Dowleh Al-e-Buyeh	
Qazi Abu Nasr b. Abdullah Farazi	4th/10th Century	At first chief judge in Fars. Later judge in Ghazneh	
Qazi Hasan b. Abdullah Farazi	4th/10th Century	Served jointly with his brother Abu Nasr. Later became sole chief judge. Married into Mard-âsâ family, who were *ra'is* of Fars.	
Qazi Abdullah b. Abu Hasan Farazi	Early 5th/11th century	Held both chief judgeship and *riyasat* by inheritance.	
Qazi Abu Taher Mohammad Fazari	d. 492/1098	Founder of Fazariyeh School in Shiraz	
Qazi Abu Mohammad Fazari	Early 6th/12th century	Chief Judge of Fars at time of composition of *Farsnameh-ye-Ibn Balkhi*	
II. Fâli-Sirâfi Family			MF, II, 297; III, 82. SA, 420–26, 442–3 SN, 172–4 TV, 96, 120, 148 IB, 195, 198
Saraj al-Din Mokarram Fali	d. 621/1223	Also *khatib* of the *Masjed-e-Now*	
Majd al-Din Esma'il Fali	d. 666/1268	Appointed by Atabek Abu Bakr to replace Seyyed Ezz al-Din Alavi	
Rokn al-Din Yahya b. Esma'il Fali	d. 707/1307	Served jointly as chief judge with Qazi Naser al-Din Beiza'i.	
Majd al-Din Esma'il b. Yahya Fali	670–756/ 1271–1355	One of Hafez's five great men of Fars under Abu Eshaq Inju	

continued

Name	Dates	Remarks	Sources
III. Alavi (Related to Fali-Sirafi)			TV, 96 SA, 292f SN, 202
Seyyed Sharaf al-Din Mohammad b. Eshaq	d. 641/1243	Son of the *naqib* of Shiraz	
Seyyed Ezz al-Din Eshaq b. Mohammad	7th/13th century	Dismissed by Atabek Abu Bakr (uncertain—could have been grandfather, also named Ezz al-Din Ebrahim)	
IV. Beizâ'i			SA, 77, 303. FNN, II, 183–4 TV, 120 SN, 182–83 Br., III, 63
Fakhr al-Din Mohammad b. Sadr al-Din Ali Beiza'I	7th/13th century		
Emam al-Din Omar b. Mohammad Beiza'I	d. 675/1276		
Naser al-Din Abdullah b. Omar Beiza'i	Uncertain. d. ca. 700/1300	Author of Nezam al-Tavarikh and Asrar al-Tanzil (an Arabic commentary on the Qoran). After 1279 held the chief judgeship jointly with Qazi Rokn al-Din Fali-Sirafi	
V. Others			SA, 345ff, 361ff K., 81 FNN, I, 59–60 TV, 93 SN, 171
Qazi Jamal al-Din Mesri	d. 653/1255	Chief judge under Atabek Abu Bakr b. Sa'd	
Qazi Borhan al-Din Fathollah	756–60/1355–59	Also minister of Amir Mohammad Mozaffar	
Baha al-Din Abu'l-Mohassen Osman b. Ali Kuhgiluyeh	767–82/1366–80	Appointed by Shah Shoja in 767/1366	

Abbreviations: Br.=E.G Browne, FN=*Farsnameh-ye-Ibn Balkhi*, TV=*Tarikh-e-Vassaf*, SA=*Shadd al-Izar*, SN=*Shiraznameh*, IB=Ibn Battuta, FNN=*Farsnameh-ye-Naseri*, K=Kotbi, MF=*Mojmal-e-Fasihi*

Fars. They lavish praise as frequently and extravagantly on judges as they do on kings and ministers. Hafez and others would never have wasted verses praising the *qazi al-qozat* if he were not a wealthy and powerful figure capable of furnishing poets with valuable patronage. Hafez composed verses praising the three great chief judges of his age. About Qazi Majd al-Din Esma'il Fali he says:

دگر مربی اسلام شیخ مجد الدین   که قاضی به ازو آسمان ندارد یاد

Another is Sheikh Majd al-Din, the leader of Islam,
Heaven cannot recall a greater judge than he.

About Borhan al-Din, the judge and minister of Amir Mohammad Mozaffar, Hafez says:

برهان ملک و دین که ز دست وزارتش   ایام کان یمین شد و دریا یسار هم

بر یاد رای انور او آسمان بصبح   جان میکند فدا و کواکب نثار هم

Borhan al-Din, whose ministry
Put the days of the earth on the right and those of the sea
    on the left.
In memory of his wise vision, the morning sky
Gives up its stars and its very life.

And on the death of Qazi Baha al-Din Osman, Shah Shoja's chief judge:

بها الحق و الدین طاب مثواه   امام سنت و شیخ جماعت

بدین دستور تاریخ وفاتش   برون آر از حروف قرب طاعت

Baha al-Din, may he rest in peace,
The imam of tradition, the sheikh of the community.
Find the date of his death thus
From the words قرب طاعت = 782/1380

LOCAL CENTERS OF POWER

The Seyyeds

In Shiraz no one but the ruler and his minister could match the personal influence of the chief judge, the *qazi al-gozat*. As a group, however, the seyyeds—or Alavis (descendents of the prophet Mohammad through his son-in-law Ali)—of Shiraz, under their leader the *naqib,* formed a large, cohesive, and influential center of power. Among Iranian cities, Shiraz was especially famous for the number and power of its *seyyeds*. In the four-teenth century, fourteen hundred of them, young and old, lived there and received stipends from the government.[41]

The *seyyeds* of Shiraz were numerous, powerful, respected, wealthy, and well-organized. As early as 982, the *naqib* prayed at the funeral of Sheikh-e-Kabir, according to the last wishes of the saint.[42] Naqibs were consid-ered noble enough to make marriage alliances with rulers. For example, Seyyed Majd al-Din Mohammad, *naqib* of Shiraz in the late thirteenth century, married the daughter of the local ruler, Sheikh Jamal al-Din Tibi Malek-e-Eslam. Naqibs and members of their families also served as judges and married into the powerful Fali-Sirafi family.[43]

The *seyyeds* of Shiraz controlled a great deal of wealth in the form of endowments. In 1309 Sultan Oljaitu founded a *Dar al-Seyyadeh* (seyyeds' lodge) in Shiraz, and endowed it with an income of 10,000 dinars a year. At that time the *naqib* of Shiraz was Ezz al-Din Ahmad (d. 1313), a mem-ber of the famous family of Musavi *seyyeds*. This *naqib* was an extremely wealthy man who endowed a seminary, freed slaves, and paid off the debts of the poor. His son, Seyyed Taj al-Din Ja'far (d. ca. 1354), held such power and prestige that no meeting could begin without him.[44]

Their wealth and prestige gave the *seyyeds* considerable independence from the ruler. One of them, Amir Asil al-Din Alavi (d. 1286), famous for his outspokenness, forced Atabek Abu Bakr to forbid Shia *ma'rakeh* (pop-ular storytelling shows) in Shiraz by threatening to leave the city. Seyyed Qazi Sharaf al-Din Mohammad (d. 1243) was both "rich and feared by rulers."[45] Apparently this *seyyed*'s family was both too rich and too feared for the ruler, and Atabek Abu Bakr dismissed the *seyyed*'s son, Seyyed Ezz al-Din Eshaq, from his position as chief judge of Fars and confiscated the wealth of many prominent Alavis.[46]

The sources do not say how the *naqib* was chosen. Like the chief judge,

Table 5.2. Naqibs of Shiraz

Name	Dates	Sources
I. Descendents of Naqib Abi Mo'ali Ja'far b. Zeid Asud.		SN, 201–2 SA, 292–4
Ezz al-Din Eshaq	Early 7th/13th century	
Qazi Sharaf al-Din Mohammad b. Eshaq	Died 641/1243	
Qazi Ezz al-Din Eshaq b. Mohammad	7th/13th century	
II. Musavi Seyyeds		SN, 205 SA, 170–2
Taj al-Din Ja'far b. Ebrahim	614–703/1217–1303	
Ezz al-Din Ahmad b. Ja'far	Died 713/1313	
Taj al-Din Ja'far b. Ahmad	Died ca. 755/1354	
III. Others		
Seyyed Abu Eshaq	Naqib at death of Sheikh al-Kabir, 371/982	SN, 153
Seyyed Nezam al-Din Ahmad	Died 530/1135	SN, 202–3
Seyyed Majd al-Din Mohammad	Died late 7th/13th Century	SA, 346–7
Abbreviations: SA=*Shadd al-Izar,* SN=*Shiraznameh.*		

the *naqib* must have gained his office through a combination of inheritance, royal appointment, and support from within the community of Shirazi *seyyed*s. Table 5.2 shows that, until the middle of the thirteenth century, the office belonged mostly to the descendents of Abu al-Mo'ali Ja'far b. Hosein b. Zeid b. Hosein b. Zeid Asud.[47] In the thirteenth and fourteenth centuries the office came into the family of the Musavi Seyyeds. Some naqibs were from neither of these families, although intermarriage among the Alavis of Shiraz may have passed the office along the female side.[48]

The *seyyed*s of Shiraz had not only a *naqib* but also subordinate, neighborhood leaders who wielded power and influence in the city. In 1353, during the Mozaffarid siege, Abu Eshaq executed the leader of the *seyyed*s of the Darb-e-Masjed-e-Now area. This execution alienated many of the Alavis of Shiraz and eased the subsequent Mozaffarid takeover. The son of this executed *seyyed,* at Amir Mohammad's order, himself executed Shah Sheikh Abu Eshaq in 1357.

Guilds, Neighborhoods, and Street Mobs

In addition to the judges and the *seyyeds,* whose chiefs sat at the top of Shirazi society, the leaders of the trade guilds and the neighborhood organizations played key roles in running the city. Any ruler making Shiraz his capital needed the support of the leaders (called *kalu,* pl. *kaluviyan*) of these groups, who were responsible for the security and the day-to-day operations of two of the most important institutions in Shiraz—the bazaar and the neighborhood. In times of siege, for example, these *kaluviyan* oversaw defense of the city wall and those city gates adjoining their neighborhoods.[49]

The neighborhood chiefs drew much of their power from their control of street mobs and from their ability to turn those mobs for or against a ruler or official. During the fourteenth century the level and frequency of mob violence increased as rival Injus, Chupanis, and Mozaffarids battled for control of the city. Both rulers and city aristocrats feared the power of the *kalus* and their mobs, and attempted to control them by a combination of force and favors. Abu Eshaq, for example, forbade the Shirazis from carrying weapons and kept them out of his personal service, preferring Esfahanis for this purpose.[50] At the same time, Kalu Fakhr, who had fought against Yaghi Basti Chupani for Abu Eshaq during the struggles of 1342, became virtual ruler of the Kazeroun Gate quarter of the city and one of the most powerful men in Shiraz.[51] Abu Eshaq's relations with other neighborhood chiefs were not always so fortunate. During the fighting of 1342, a certain Kalu Hosein took the side of the Chupanis. Ten years later, during the Mozaffarid siege of Shiraz, Abu Eshaq alienated some of the *kaluviyan* by executing the chief of the Bagh-e-Now district and plotting against the chief of the Murdestan quarter. These shortsighted actions led the latter to betray the city to the Mozaffarids.

In the streets and bazaars of Shiraz there existed an undercurrent of resistance to almost all rulers, which though occasionally expressed in violence, most often appeared as a sullen, passive opposition using weapons of mockery and ridicule—at which Shirazis have always excelled. For example, a certain Shah Asheq (whose very name parodied Abu Eshaq's title of Shah Sheikh) kept a candy store near the door of the Old Congregational Mosque. This storekeeper composed poetry in Shirazi dialect and had a reputation in the city as something of a wit. One Friday, after Abu Eshaq had finished his prayers at the mosque, the ruler came and sat in the shop and told his officers and courtiers, "Today I am Shah Asheq's shopkeeper—come and buy candy from me." Each officer offered rich clothes, weapons, and cash in return for candy until 100,000 dinars worth of goods and cash had been collected. Abu Eshaq, who considered himself a second Hatam Tai (an Arab chief legendary for his generosity), then mounted his horse and left the treasure for the shop owner. Shah Asheq, however, trumped the king's generosity by announcing from the roof of his shop, "O people of Shiraz, the king has given me gifts and I will donate them for the king to the people of Shiraz. Come and loot my shop." The Shirazis looted Shah Asheq's store, and when the king found out what had happened, he could only admit that a Shirazi shopkeeper had bested him.[52]

Relations between the *bazaaris* of Shiraz and the Mozaffarid rulers were not much better. When Amir Mohammad and his escort passed through the bazaars, they found their way blocked by piles of firewood the shopkeepers deliberately left in the passages. In general, the neighborhood chiefs of Shiraz favored Shah Shoja over the other members of his family. After Shah Mahmud, with Jalayerid support, had taken Shiraz from his brother in 1364, the Shirazis sent Kalu Hasan on a mission to Shah Shoja in Kerman. There he appealed to Shah Shoja to return to Shiraz and promised him support in return for relief from the exactions of Shah Mahmud's Tabrizi allies.[53] Two years later, Shah Mahmud, fearing the *kalus* of Shiraz would betray him to Shah Shoja, abandoned the city to his brother and withdrew to Esfahan.

Below the *kaluviyan,* and presumably controlled by them, were the urban workers and potential members of street mobs. These groups, whom the aristocrats called by the disparaging names of *rendan, owbash,* and *shattar,* attained their greatest strength during the reign of Abu Eshaq. The Mozaffarids earned the gratitude of the Shirazi aristocrats by suppressing the street mobs and restoring security.[54]

These young men of Shiraz gloried in the titles *pahlavan* and *javanmard* (hero, strong man); the upper classes called these same workers of the bazaar owbash (ruffians). By their ideals, the *pahlavanan* upheld *javanmardi* (chivalry), and their societies offered hospitality to the stranger and protection to the weak in a violent society.[55] For example, in 1339 Tashi Khatun, the mother of Abu Eshaq, appealed to the *javanmardi* of the bazaar workers of Shiraz, and in response a carpenter named Pahlavan Mahmud started a revolt against Amir Pir Hosein Chupani.[56] Although the sources do not mention any specific organizations of the *javanmardan* or *pahlavanan* in Shiraz, Ibn Battuta mentions societies of young, unmarried men in Esfahan who competed in giving festivals as extravagant as possible. The upper-class bias of the sources, however, and the semisecret nature of these popular societies, have obscured the true character of these organizations in Shiraz.

Sheikhs and Their Families

In addition to *qazis*, *naqibs* and *kalus*, who wielded power through official or semiofficial positions, others with no official position possessed great influence in Shiraz. This latter group drew its authority from the respect of the population or the ruler for an individual's family, learning, wealth, or piety. The Baghnovi family, for example, held no official post in Shiraz, but one family member, Sheikh Haj Rokn al-Din Mansur Baghnovi (d. 1333), was so blunt in his threats and advice to rulers that he earned the popular nickname *Rastgu* (the truth-speaker).[57] Another Baghnovi, Rokn al-Din's brother Sheikh Zahir al-Din Esma'il (d. 1330), led the Shirazis' resistance to Sultan Oljaitu's attempt to impose a Shia form of the *khotbeh* (Friday prayer address) in 1310.[58]

Sheikh, which originally in Arabic meant "old man," in this period was the title of leaders of the sufis and of eminent preachers. The sheikh al-eslam, the most pious and learned of the sheikhs, and those persons called sheikh al-eslam in Shiraz, were most famous as sufi leaders and preachers.[59] Judging by Hafez's inclusion of a sheikh al-eslam among his five great men of Fars, that individual, whatever his function, must have had great, if unofficial, influence over the religious community and the people of Shiraz. The most famous sheikh al-eslams of Shiraz included Qotb al-Din Ali al-Makki and his son, Shahab al-Din Ruzbehan, in the twelfth century C.E.;[60] Sheikh Ezz al-Din Mowdud Zarkub (d. 1265), the ancestor of the author of the *Shiraznameh;* Sheikh Amin al-Din Baliyani Kazeruni (d. 1344), one of Hafez's five great men of Fars; and Sheikh Farid al-Din Abd al-Wodud of the Ruzbehan Farid family in the middle of the fourteenth century.[61]

The strongest social group in Shiraz and the base of the city's cultural and social life were the fifteen to twenty aristocratic families that produced most of the city's judges, teachers, scholars, and preachers. These figures made fourteenth-century Shiraz into the Dar al-Elm (abode of knowledge) and the Borj-e-Owliya (tower of saints) of the Islamic world. Joneid Shirazi's *Shadd al-Izar* (written ca. 1389) contains biographies of over three hundred famous persons buried in Shiraz. Although Joneid included a few notices of rulers, ministers, and governors, he wrote mostly of religious figures—saints, scholars, martyrs, and the like.[62]

About a third of those persons whom Joneid recorded in *Shadd al-Izar* belonged to the fifteen or twenty leading families of the city. We have already seen how the chief judgeship of Fars for centuries remained in the related families of Afzari and Fali-Sirafi. Similarly, lesser posts such as those of teacher *(modarres)* and preacher *(va'ez)* usually stayed within a family. Although outsiders with talent or credentials could earn respect in religious scholarship and teaching, the advantage usually lay with scions of local families that already enjoyed the support of a ruler or minister. Whatever the merits of outsiders, the powerful Shirazi families often passed on scholarly occupations by heredity.

Table 5.3 (pp. 94–95) lists the aristocratic families of Shiraz, showing their origins and intermarriages, while the appendix gives their genealogies. The information reveals some central features of Shirazi society.

> Many leading families in the city held landholdings in the districts of Fars. The Baghnovis and Ruzbehans of Fasa, the Falis from the garmsirat near the Persian Gulf, and the three prominent families from the Beiza area originated as provincial landowners who kept their ties with the countryside after migrating to Shiraz. The family of Baliyani-Kazerouni, for example, maintained especially close links with its place of origin, and members of this family continued to be buried in Kazeroun even after attaining eminence in Shiraz.[63]

> Two aristocratic families, the Zarkubs and the Salehanis, were immigrants from Esfahan, which had suffered a decline relative to Shiraz in the thirteenth and fourteenth centuries.

Families of *seyyed*s occupied a prominent position among the Shiraz aristocrats.

Ethnically, some families, such as the prolific and powerful Baghnovis, boasted of Arab origins, although they had been thoroughly Persianized by their long residence in Fasa before settling in Shiraz.

Other families, such as the Falis of the *garmsir,* the Sheikhs of Beiza, and the Ruzbehans of Fasa, were either descendents of the old Iranian Zoroastrian *dehqan*s (landed aristocrats) of Fars or descended from Deilamite immigrants to Fars of the Buyid era.[64]

The family of Najib al-Din Ali b. Bozghash was just the most famous of the descendents of the Turks who settled in Shiraz during the Seljuq and Mongol periods.

Almost the entire religious establishment of Shiraz—the preachers, the judges, the teachers, the sufi leaders, and the sheikh al-eslam—came from these fifteen or twenty aristocratic families. Important religious figures in Shiraz who were not members of these families would establish links with the local aristocrats, usually as students of some and teachers of others. The great Shiraz families extended their influence by intermarriage, and through teacher-student or sufi master-follower relationships. The influence of Sheikh Sadr al-Din Mozaffar Baghnovi, for example, extended not only to his numerous children, grandchildren, and in-laws, but also to his many students. A teacher's possession of an *ejazeh* (diploma) from a Baghnovi conferred on him some of the same prestige that others acquired by marrying into the family.

Some of these aristocrats were more aristocratic than others. Shiraz had two tiers of first families: the elite and the local aristocracy. Among the former were the families of Fali-Sirafi, Afzari, Musavi, and Qazi Beiza'i, which gave Shiraz its chief judges, *naqib*s, and even ministers. Many members of these families were eminent scholars and teachers, but their real power was political, extending beyond the limits of Shiraz and Fars. These elite families almost never intermarried with the local aristocrats.[65] The first group included figures of international stature, while the second, although possessing considerable prestige and wealth, and holding posts

Table 5.3. Patrician Families of Shiraz

Family	Origins	Remarks	Sources
The Elite			
Afzari (Fazari)	From Afar, in the *garmsir* of Fars	Chief judges of Fars since Buyid times. Related to Fali-Sirafi family	FN 135–40 SA 358–60 SN 151
Qazi Beiza'i	Beiza of Fars	Chief judges of Fars in the 7th/13th century	SA 77, 294–5 SN 182; TV 120
Fali-Sirafi	From the region of Fal near the Persian Gulf port of Siraf. Descended from Afzari judges	Chief judges of Fars in the 13th and 14th centuries. Intermarried with families of ministers and *naqibs*. Buried in *Mosalla* area north of the city.	SA 420–44 SN 89, 172–4, 192–3, 202 TV 92, 96, 120, 148 MF II, 297, III, 73, 82. IB 195ff; HM 151
Musavi Seyyeds	Descended from Imam Musa Kazem	*Naqibs* of Fars in the 13th and 14th centuries	SA 170–74 SN 205
Local Aristocrats			
Adib-Salehani	Salehan Quarter of Esfahan	Migrated to Shiraz ca. 600/1204	SA 139, 149 SN 168–9
Alavi-Mohammadi	Seyyeds descended from Mohammad Hanafiyeh b. Ali b. Abi Taleb	Amir Asil al-Din Alavi (d. 1286) related through daughters and sisters to families of Va'ez, Arabshah-Hoseini, and Baghnovi	SA 128, 325–30 SN 204–5 MF II, 364
Baghnovi	Originally from Fasa. Descended from Caliph Omar. Settled in Bagh-e-Now area of Shiraz in the 12th century	Intermarried with families of: Kasa'i, Zarkub, Alavi-Mohammadi, Salmani, and Beiza'i. Very large and wealthy family. Preachers the Jame' Atiq. Joneid Shirazi, poet and author of *Shadd al-Izar,* member of this family.	SA 183–89, 190–210, 227–238, 268, 289–92 SN 178–80, 190
Beiza'i (Sheikhs of Beiza)	Descended from *Sheikh al-Shoyukh* Abu al-Hosein Ahmad b. Moham-mad Beiza'i (d. 1024) known as Ibn Salbeh	Most of family buried in Beiza. Descendant of Sheikh Mohammad was sufi master of Sheikh Ruzbe-han Baqli. Another descendant married Sadr al-Din Mozaffar Baghnovi (13th century).	SA 299–300, 476 ff SN 148–9, 154
Mosalahi-Beiza'i	From Beiza of Fars. Came to Shiraz in the 12th century	At first family members buried in *Dar al-Salm* cemetary. In 13th century, as family gained prestige, buried in the *Jame' Atiq* district	SA 140–43, 330–33 SN 163–4

continued

Family	Origins	Remarks	Sources
Baliyani-Kazerouni	From Baliyan, a village 6 miles south of Kazeroun. Descended from Abu Ali Daqqaq Nishapuri, (d. 1015)	Most of family buried in Kazeroun. Family of scholars and *Sheikh al-Eslams* of Fars in the 14th century.	SA 61–4, 484–87 SN 186–7, 194 K 35, FNN II, 255 B 150–54
Bozghash	Bozghash was a Turkish merchant who settled in Shiraz in Salghurid times	Family of eminent teachers, including teacher of historian Mo'in al-Din Zarkub	SA 334–41 SN 177, 191 TV 112–113
Dashtaki Seyyeds	Descended from Hosein b. Ali b. Hosein b. Ali b. Abi Taleb	Ancestors of founder of the *Man-suriyeh* School and of the author of *Farsnameh-ye-Naseri*. Intermarried with Alavi-Mohammadis	SA 300–303, 319–24 SN 204 FNN II, 80
Kasa'i	Unknown	Intermarried with Baghnovis. Founded Robat-e-Kasa'i outside the Kazerun Gate	SA 117–18, 129 SN 184–5
Ruzbehan Baqli	Descendants of Sheikh Ruzbehan Baqli *Shattah-e-Fars* (1127–1209). Of Deilamite origin from Fasa.	Ruzbehan the greatest mystic of Shiraz. Descendents were chief of *Ruzbehaniyeh* dervishes. Intermarried with Zarkubs	SA 238–39, 243–54 SN 129, 159, 162
Ruzbehan Farid	Descendants of Sheikh Ruzbehan Farid (d. 1221)	Family of *mohtasebs* and Sheikh al-Islams in the 13th and 14th centuries	SA 352–54, 394–5 SN 180–1
Salmani	Unknown: Descendants of Faqih Sa'en al-Din Hosein (d. 1266)	Intermarried with Baghnovis	SA 176–79 SN 174
Va'ez	Unknown	Married into Alavi-Mohammadi family. Eminent preachers in the 14th century	SA 128
Zarkub (Zahabi)	From Esfahan. Descendants of Hafez Esma'il Qavam al-Sonnat (d. 1140)	Migrated to Shiraz in the 13th century. Family of *Sheikh al-Eslams* and of historian Ahmad Zarkub. Intermarried with Ruzbehan Baqlis	SA 310–19

Abbreviations: SA = *Shadd al-Izar*; SN = *Shiraznameh*; TV = *Tarikh-e-Vassaf*; MF = *Mojmal-e-Fasihi*; IB = *Ibn Battuta*; FN = *Farsnameh-ye-Ibn Balkhi*; FNN = *Farsnameh-ye-Naseri*; HM = *Hezar Mazar*; K = *Kotbi*; B = *Bulliet* in the important seminaries, mosques, and sufi orders of the city, were usually limited in power and influence to Shiraz and Fars.

Despite frequent intermarriage among the second-tier local aristocrats, there were important distinctions of power and prestige within this group. The most eminent of the local aristocrats were the families of Baghnovi, Dashtaki, and Alavi-Mohammadi, and sheikhs of Beiza, while at the lower end of the aristocratic scale were the families of Zarkub, Va'ez, Kasa'i, and Adib-Salehani.[66] Members of these "lower aristocratic" families were often preachers and imams in the smaller mosques of the city.[67] They could raise their status by attaching themselves (by marriage or other means) to more prominent families. Politically, these lower aristocratic families were closest to the *kalus* and their neighborhood and bazaar organizations, while the higher group had ties both with the neighborhood chiefs and with the ruling elite of ministers, governors, and judges.

CONCLUSION: AN INTERLOCKING DIRECTORATE

The sources draw a picture of fourteenth-century Shiraz that is not one of orderly hierachies, pyramids and webs. Rather, it is a picture of overlapping and undefined jurisdictions that changed according to the personalities of the holders of various offices. It mattered less *what* you were than *who* you (and your relatives) were. At the top of society was the ruler or governor—always an outsider, aloof from Shiraz and its people. Change of ruler or even of dynasty seldom directly affected life in the city. The minister took a closer interest in the city by looking to both physical security (by means of his police force) and economic prosperity in the town and countryside, in order to ensure that his tax collectors could gather enough cash revenue to fill the ruler's treasury and pay his troops.

The real authority touching Shirazis was that of the chief judge, the *qazi al-qozat*. Although usually from one of the great families of Shiraz, the chief judge had so much political power and wealth in land that his interests coincided with those of an alien ruling class. The *naqib*, thanks to the wealth he controlled and the prestige of his office, ranked only slightly below the chief judge. Sometimes the two offices were held by the same person, or by close relatives. Together they were the top drawer of the Shirazi establishment, representing stability and permanence in an age of frequent, violent political change.

Ranking below the chief judge and *naqib*, but still with considerable local influence, were the aristocratic Shirazi families of scholars, *sheikh al-eslams*, preachers, and sufi leaders. The *kaluviyan* of the bazaars and neighborhoods lacked the prestige of the aristocrats but often held greater actual power. Further down the social scale were the *pahlavanan* and their secret societies—street ruffians or popular heroes, depending on one's point of view.

All of these groups and individuals stood in vague, undefined relationships to each other. Many young aristocrats were students of eminent judges, and many judges studied as young men under teachers who were not their families' social equals. The *kalus* of Shiraz had links both downward, with the *pahlavans*, and upward, with the aristocratic families. The most powerful of the *kalus*, such as Kalu Fakhr of the Kazeroun Gate quarter, had connections even at the ruler's court, where ministers and princes would compete for their favor and support.

The most important feature of this system (or nonsystem) of city organization is that it did work to preserve Shiraz. Given the political instability of Iran in the fourteenth century, Shiraz's economic survival and cultural flowering were major accomplishments. Occasional breakdowns of order and security never threatened Shiraz's existence as a city. The network of formal and informal ties among the different groups of Shirazis meant that most of the inhabitants—from the *rend* in the tavern to the ascetic in his cell—shared an interest in their city's survival. Add to this common interest an intense local patriotism and pride, and the result was a loose, but strong, social structure in which all could share Hafez's sentiments when he said:

خوشا شیراز و وضع بی مثالش   خداوندا نگهدار از زوالش

Pleasant is Shiraz and its incomparable site. O Lord, preserve it
   from decline.

6

Shirazi Society: Patricians, Poets, and Scholars

[Hafez] reflected the life as it had been spun for the people of Iran for two thousand years. He did so with such precision, that when, today, we drink of his lyrics it is as if we are drinking of history

—M. A. Eslami-Nodushan
The Eternal Story of Hafez

In Hafez's Shiraz, rulers, ministers, and judges took power directly from their offices. One judge might be more or less powerful than another, but there was no question about what a judge *was supposed* to do. Below these top officials, however, the picture was different. Nowhere was the power of the *kalu,* the *pahlavan,* the teacher, and the sufi *sheikh* clearly defined. All of these persons, however—with or without job descriptions—had a share in running the city. In the last chapter we indicated something of how they did it. Beyond city administration, a crucial question remains: how did the Shirazis interact as individuals and groups and what kind of society did they form by their interactions? By extension, what manner of society formed the setting for Hafez's beautiful lyrics?

Hafez's Shiraz was above all a religious society, where the beliefs, culture and practices of Islam shaped every aspect of social life. This religious society, despite the best efforts of a strict ruler like Mohammad Mozaffar, was never puritanical, full of only somber prayers and fasts. Few Iranians of any faith have ever been full-time puritans or ascetics, and their all-embracing Islam has included widely varying beliefs and practices. The Islamic society of Hafez's Shiraz was not straitlaced, but as rich and diverse as the Iranian imagination itself.

THE MYSTERY OF CITY FACTIONS

The factions in medieval Islamic cities are a mysterious yet crucial problem for the social historian. Why, in a given city at a given time, did one group fight another? And why, at another time or place, were there no outbreaks of factional strife? Feuding groups (called *asabiyat*) were most prevalent in the cities of Iran during the pre-Mongol era, and were strongest in the towns of Khorasan. In the tenth century there were few places in that province without factions: the populations of Nishapur, Sarakhs, Herat, Marv, and others were divided into rival parties based on religion, law school, neighborhood, or some other principle of allegiance.[1]

This factional division could lead to bloody street fighting. In the middle of the twelfth century, open warfare between Shafi'is and Hanafis left Nishapur in ruins more than half a century before the arrival of the Mongol armies.[2] The Mongols, by slaughtering members of all factions indiscriminately, ended much of the feuding in Khorasan. By the fourteenth century, the intensity of the factionalism of the earlier period was gone. In this later period, Esfahan was most famous for violent factional disputes (called in Persian *do-hava'i*). Even there, these disputes were considered a survival of earlier practices that had died out elsewhere. According to Mostowfi, writing in the fourteenth century:

> Most of the people of Esfahan are Sunni of the Shafi'i school and observe religion exactly. But most of the time they fight and argue, for the custom of feuding *(do-hava'i)* has never disappeared from here.[3]

According to Mostowfi's account, the fighting in Esfahan was based not on opposing law schools, but on some (unknown) issue that provoked strife among the city quarters. He notes the verse:

تا در دشت هست و جوباره   نیست از کشتن و کشش چاره

As long as Dardasht and Jubareh exist,
There will be endless strife and slaughter.[4]

In the fourteenth century this custom of *do-hava'i* did not extend into Fars and Shiraz. In a revealing passage describing the town of Qomisheh (later Shahreza), Mostowfi says that this town had been formerly part of Esfahan province *(Eraq-e-Ajam)* and was in his time considered the northernmost town of Fars. He adds, "Its people are temperamentally like the Esfahanis, and here the custom of factional disputes persists."[5] At the death of Shah Mahmud Mozaffari in 1374, factionalism reappeared in Esfahan, as two groups of the inhabitants, called *chahar-dangeh* (two-thirds) and *do-dangeh* (one-third), fought over a successor.[6] Kerman also saw fighting between natives, who supported Makhdum Shah Khan Qotlogh, the mother of Shah Shoja, and the Khorasanis, who supported Pahlavan Asad, the governor of the city.[7]

This phenomenon appears in Shiraz in the late eighteenth and nineteenth centuries, when the five northern and eastern quarters were called *Heidarikhaneh* and the five western and southern quarters were called *Ne'-matikhaneh*. According to the nineteenth century *Farsnameh-ye-Naseri,* this division dated from Safavid times, when the rulers, on the principle of "divide and rule," split cities and villages into eastern (Heidari) and western (Ne'mati) districts. This custom resulted in three or four bloody riots a year between the rival groups in Shiraz, until the Qajar rulers suppressed the fighting in the middle of the nineteenth century. According to this account, the Heidari faction took its name from Sheikh Heidar Safavi (r. 1456–88), father of Shah Esma'il, and the Ne'mati from Shah Ne'matol-lah Vali of Kerman (d. 1431).[8]

There is no evidence of permanent factions in Shiraz before the Safavids. The sources mention two instances in the fourteenth century, when the neighborhood chiefs and other nobles split into rival groups whose adherents fought in the streets.

The first incident occurred in 1342 following the murder of Mas'ud Shah Inju by the Chupanid Amir Yaghi Basti. The city population divided between supporters of Yaghi Basti and Abu Eshaq Inju, who had arisen to avenge his brother's murder. Supporting the Injus were some of the most powerful figures of Shiraz, including Khwajeh Qavam al-Din Hasan, one of Hafez's "five nobles" of Fars, who later became Abu Eshaq's minister and closest advisor; Khwajeh Fakhr al-Din Salmani, a member of the powerful Salmani family;[9] Jamal al-Din Khasseh, a member of another powerful local family;[10] and Kalu Fakhr, chief of the Kazeroun Gate quarter. Supporters of Yaghi Basti included a certain Kalu Hosein and the nobles of the quarter where the Mongol governor was located. The two sides battled in the streets for twenty days until the Inju partisans received outside help and expelled the Chupanids from the city.[11]

The second outbreak of factional violence in Shiraz occurred in 1354, when the inhabitants of the Kazeroun Gate quarter joined a Shulestani army in an attempt to retake the city for Abu Eshaq. Together these pro-Inju forces temporarily expelled the Mozaffarid ruler and attacked the Murdestan quarter, whose chief, Kalu Omar, had originally betrayed the city to Amir Mohammad's army. Only the arrival of Shah Shoja and his forces preserved the city for the Mozaffarids, who dealt a bloody defeat to Abu Eshaq's partisans. The fighting did not end until the Mozaffarids and their Shirazi allies had destroyed the Kazeroun Gate quarter and massacred all rebel prisoners.[12]

The sources do not suggest that these outbreaks of factional violence in fourteenth-century Shiraz originated in fundamental divisions in the society, such as Islamic law school or neighborhood.[13] If permanent rival factions had existed in the city, the fighting described above would have been based on social and economic class divisions, ethnic or religious differences, or on some unknown principle of allegiance. In Shiraz, there was no principle at stake, and these isolated outbreaks of violence pitting neighborhood against neighborhood were most likely not the result of permanent divisions or deep-rooted ideological differences between the battling parties.[14] Rather, they occurred when competing Shirazi groups and individuals were drawn into the struggles of rival contenders for high office.[15]

SOCIAL LIFE

Iranians have always mixed the religious, economic, and social parts of their lives, and the inhabitants of a city that called itself "the tower of saints" (borj al-owliya) could never separate the religious from the secular. The Shirazi "saint" (vali, pl. owliya) did not withdraw from the realities of daily life.

He was an integral part of urban society, whether involved in commerce, scholarship, or the fine arts. In fourteenth-century Shiraz, he was very much a part of the everyday world. Although often choosing holy poverty, he would seldom beg, but would practice some modest means of livelihood. The sources suggest that to find the saint one should search not only in mosques and dervish cells, but also in the shops of the bazaar, where he would be found working behind a set of scales weighing merchandise.[16]

Pilgrimage

Pilgrimage to the tombs of saints was one of the bases of social life in Hafez's Shiraz. Pilgrimage for the Shirazis, however, was never an act of dry, zealous piety. The Moslem pilgrim, much like his English contemporary in the *Canterbury Tales,* enjoyed pilgrimage as an opportunity to socialize with friends, meet different people, view the spectacle of the great shrines, and partake of the food and drink provided there. Pilgrims could see a spectacular display at the shrine of Ahmad b. Musa every Sunday between afternoon and evening prayers, when Tashi Khatun, the mother of Abu Eshaq, would visit the tomb. While the Khatun watched from an adjoining pavilion, *seyyed*s, scholars, and judges would gather to hear the recitations of the finest Qoran-readers of Shiraz while being served fruit, sweets, and other dishes. Then a preacher would ascend the pulpit and deliver a sermon. Finally, trumpets, horns, and drums sounded at the gate of the shrine, just as was done before a king's palace.[17]

Once a week, eminent Shirazis would gather at the tomb of Ibn Khafif, Sheikh-e-Kabir, in the Darb-e-Estakhr quarter. Tashi Khatun would also visit this shrine every Thursday evening. Here the ceremony was much more modest, and the pilgrims simply rubbed their hands on the grave.[18] A popular place of pilgrimage for students was the grave of Sibawayh the Grammarian (d. 796). Those hoping to learn Arabic grammar would rub their chests against the gravestone, today known as Sang-e-Siyah, the black stone.[19]

The Shirazis buried many of their dead inside the city, and thus small places of pilgrimage were scattered through the residential areas of the town. At someone's death, the members of the family would often bury him or her in one of the rooms of the house and convert that room into a small shrine. They would spread mats and carpets in the room, light candles at the head and foot of the grave, and place a door with an iron-grated window leading directly from the room to the street so that Qoran-readers could enter. The family would take care of this tomb by keeping it carpeted and its lamps lit. They would also give the deceased's share of a meal as alms for the sake of his soul.[20]

For a site to become a frequented place of pilgrimage, it was not always necessary for a famous person to be buried there. By the fourteenth century, the identity of saints buried at many famous shrines had been forgotten, and the shrines bore only popular names unrelated to their true occupants. A pilgrimage site might also arise around the site of a miracle. The garden of *Haft-tanan* (the bodies of seven saints), which today stands just north of the tomb of Hafez, originated this way. According to a fourteenth-century account in *Shadd al Izar,* one night a handsome young dervish led to the site a pious undertaker who lived near the Estakhr gate. In the undertaker's account:

> I accompanied him to a walled area in the Mosalla district, which was known as *Samdal* in those days. Then that young man said, "Wait here." I waited for an hour and suddenly I heard *Allahu Akbar.* I went in and found that young man dead and laid out facing the Qebleh. . . . I was astonished and was wondering how I would wash and bury him alone, when suddenly six others appeared bringing winding-sheets. They came and helped me prepare him for burial, then picked him up and took him outside the building. I could not follow them, so I washed and dressed and went out. I saw there was no wall or barrier, and wherever I looked were open fields and no sign of anyone. I sat and prayed, and then slept. When I awoke in the morning I saw a new grave there, freshly watered. I suspected it must have been the young man's grave.[21]

The author of *Shadd Al-Izar* adds: "After a short time, other graves appeared next to this one until finally there were seven. No one knew the identity of the seven companions, and today [i.e., late fourteenth century] the graves are marked with seven blank stones."

Dreams and Miracles
Those persons in Shiraz who foretold the future, controlled the *jenn* (spirits), and interpreted dreams occupied a very important place in society.

Their clients included the most powerful men of the city. One of these seers was Faqih Jamal al-Din Hosein (d. fourteenth century), called *mo'abber,* the dream interpreter.[22] In a vision, the Shiraz saint Ahmab b. Musa (today's Shah-e-Cheragh) led him to the prophet Joseph (in Islam known as Yusef Sadigh), who bestowed upon Jamal al-Din the gift of dream interpretation. One of his most famous clients was the *naqib* of Shiraz, Majd al-Din Mohammad, who consulted the *mo'abber* about an erotic dream. When Seyyed Majd al-Din was ashamed to relate his dream, the interpreter guessed what it was, and, in return for a gift of 1,000 dinars (in advance), told him he would make a great and advantageous marriage. As it happened, this *naqib* later married the daughter of the ruler of Shiraz, Jamal al-Din Tibi Malek-e-Eslam.[23]

Shiraz also contained miracle workers and persons who could "understand secrets." The historian Faqih Sa'en al-Din Hosein Salmani (d. 1266) was known as *mofti al-jenn* because he could summon and command the spirits of the supernatural world.[24] A certain Sheikh Zein al-Din Ali Kolah, a contemporary of the translator of *Shadd al-Izar,* was also famous for his ability to capture and control the *jenn.*[25]

No class had a monopoly on miracle-working in this period; persons with supernatural powers appeared among both the aristocrats (see, for example, Qazi Majd al-Din's miraculous escape from the sultan's dogs in chapter 5) and the common people. Sheikh Shams al-Din Mohammad Sadeq (d. 1336) began as a common, illiterate man. Suddenly and miraculously he became learned, and earned great respect from the scholars of Shiraz.[26] A certain Sheikh Ali Laban (d. 1377) was a poor brickmaker who would attend meetings of scholars and had holy visions. He also understood secrets and could foretell the future. Once a man came to him complaining that his wife was disobedient but that he was too poor to divorce her and too fearful of God's wrath to kill her. The Sheikh told him, "Give something to the poor and on Wednesday you will be free of this woman." On the following Wednesday the man returned and said, "She is not dead." The sheikh answered, "It is still Wednesday." When the man returned to his house he saw his wife fall off the roof and die.[27]

Asceticism and Its Opposite

Few cities combined so much hedonism and so much spiritualism as Shiraz. As far as the government was concerned, the dissipations of the *ren-*

dan were preferable to the fasts of the *zahedan* or ascetics.[28] For, while the latter worked at the simplest jobs and paid few taxes, the former were steady customers of the *kharabat* (vice-dens) of the city—the brothels *(beit al-lotf)*, wine-shops *(sharabkhaneh)*, opium dens *(bangkhaneh)*, and gambling houses *(qomarkhaneh)*—all of which, if we can believe the fifteenth-century inscription cited earlier, paid *tamgha* to the treasury.[29] The rulers, except for the strict Amir Mobarez al-Din Mohammad Mozaffar (nicknamed *mohtaseb,* or inspector), taxed rather than suppressed the *rendans'* activities, in spite of the opposition of the ascetics and other religious groups.

In the conflict between asceticism and hedonism, Hafez was firmly on the side of the latter, praising the hedonists' freedom from and indifference to respectable opinion. In one of his verses, Hafez has beautifully captured the disdain of the *rendan* for the opinion of others, while showing the heart of the opposition between *rendi* (hedonism) and *zohd* (asceticism).

عیب رندان مکن ای زاهد پاکیزه سرشت   که گناه دگران بر تو نخواهد گرفت

من گر نیکم و گر بد برو خود را باش   هر کس آن درود عاقبت کار که کاشت

Do not criticize the *rendan,* O pure ascetic.
For you will not be charged with the sins of others.
Whether I am good or evil—you go and be yourself;
In the end everyone will reap what he sows.

The wine that the *rendan* drank at their taverns was stronger stuff than "the mystic symbol of divine love."[30] Hafez himself was a connoisseur who knew that good wine turned pale with aging. In the following verse he compares old, pale wine with someone frightened of the *mohtaseb.*[31]

شراب خانگی ترس محتسب دیده

Home-made wine frightened [turned pale] by the inspector.

Both the ascetics with their fasts and the *rendan* with their debaucheries were integral parts of life in Hafez's Shiraz. According to Mostowfi, the Shirazis were "much addicted to holy poverty," and were, for the most part, content to do just enough trade to avoid begging.[32] Shiraz's ascetics had different ways of withdrawing from the world, from the most personal and modest to the most extreme and ostentatious. One of the Baghnovi family, for example, went on pilgrimage secretly so that the people would not call him *haji*.[33] Mowlana Nezam al-Din Esma'il Khorasani (d. 1228) refused to accept the post of *modarres* (chief instructor) of the Fakhriyeh Seminary, but taught there instead as an ordinary scholar.[34] At the far end of the ascetic scale was a certain Sheikh Rostam Khorasani (d. 1340), who lived in the *rabat* of Sheikh-e-Kabir. He would eat nothing in the *rabat,* but would beg his food every evening, accepting only what the people put into his mouth.[35]

Some members of the most powerful and wealthy Shirazi families would withdraw into asceticism. The son of the *naqib* of Shiraz, Seyyed Nosrat al-Din Ali b. Ahmad Musavi (d. fourteenth century) spent his life in seclusion, performing one thousand prayer prostrations every twenty-four hours. It was said that in his entire life he never saw the countryside or a tree, and when they asked him, "Is a fig tree larger or a cucumber tree?" he answered, "The cucumber." When they told him that the opposite was true, he exclaimed, "Then praise God almighty who has made the large small and the small large!"[36]

If all Shirazis had been ascetics the city would not have survived economically. Nor would it have survived physically if all the inhabitants had been *rendan.* Most Shirazis were neither, but could accept the existence of both as part of their community. The great strength of Shirazi society was its diversity—its ability to absorb a variety of human behavior without collapsing under the strains of disparate, conflicting groups. In fact, the city did not merely tolerate but valued this diversity, since the presence of so many different kinds of people—drunkards, ascetics, poets, preachers, and others—gave Shiraz a rich and varied life that encouraged the cultural flowering of the fourteenth century and inspired so many powerful images in Hafez.[37]

Shi'ism

Shi'ism was one religious current in fourteenth-century Shiraz, but its exact status there, like the entire history of Shi'ism in pre-Safavid Iran, is surrounded with questions.[38] In the fourteenth century, "twelver" Shi'ism (which would become the state religion of Iran in the sixteenth century) predominated in only a few areas of central Iran, mostly in the districts of the second-rank towns of Rey, Varamin, Qom, Kashan, Tafresh, and Nahavand. The sources report that Shiraz, like most of the major towns, had few Shia inhabitants.[39]

We know there were Shia in Shiraz thanks to the activities of their opponents, the most adamant of whom were the Alavi patricians. Both the austere Amir Asil al-Din Abdullah Alavi-Mohammadi (d. 1286) and his grandson (through his daughter), Amir Seyyed Taj al-Din Mohammad b. Heidar Dashtaki-Shirazi (d. 1363), spoke and wrote against the Shia, the former threatening to leave Shiraz unless the Salghurid ruler suppressed Shi'ite books and *ma'rakeh* (street performances of Shia traditions).[40]

Although the evidence is not conclusive, the Shi'ism that existed in Shiraz and Fars could have been a lower class or rural movement.[41] Among some elements of society in this period there existed the expectation of the coming of the *mahdi* or messiah, whose appearance, in the form of the hidden Imam, is part of Shi'a doctrine. Certainly the unsettled political and social climate of fourteenth-century Iran contributed to such expectations. In Fars the sources record two incidents involving a purported *mahdi* during the Il-Khanid period. In 1265, a certain Seyyed Sharaf al-Din Ebrahim claimed to be the *mahdi* and led a revolt which was put down by Mongol troops.[42] In the second recorded incident, a Sheikh Shams al-Din Omar Mashhadi came to Shiraz around 1300, where he preached so effectively that some of his followers claimed he was the *mahdi;* the authorities executed him out of fear of popular religious disturbances.[43]

In the thirteenth and fourteenth centuries, what are today the major Shi'ite shrines of Shiraz were ecumenical. They existed and flourished as centers of pilgrimage in a Sunni setting. In those days, even the ultra-orthodox Salghurids, famous for their opposition to Shi'ism, endowed and venerated tombs of the family of Musa Kazem, the eighth Imam of the Shia.[44]

A little more than a century after Hafez's death, when Shah Esma'il Safavi made Shi'ism the state religion of his empire, the Shirazis found themselves well-equipped to convert their most important shrines into centers of Shia pilgrimage and devotion. Today these same tombs link Shiraz to Shi'ism, and place Shiraz just behind Mashhad and Qom as pilgrimage sites for Shia believers from inside and outside Iran. In particular, the grave of Ahmad b. Musa, brother of the eighth Imam and popularly known as Shah-e-Cheragh, is a major shrine of the Shia world.

Academic and Social Relations

In Hafez's Shiraz, known in the sources as *Dar al-Elm* (abode of learning), thousands of scholars studied and taught. In such a setting, the relation between teacher and student was a key element of urban social life. In the fourteenth century, like today, society often described a person in terms of the quality and quantity of his education. While today we define this education in terms of the institution attended and degree earned, Hafez and his contemporaries would have defined it in terms of one's teachers and the books studied. A scholar studied a work or works with a specific teacher, and the greater the teacher, the greater the prestige of his students. A diploma, or *ejazeh,* received from a famous teacher specifying what that student had learned (for example, ten chapters of book A and all of Book B) was a precious document for a young scholar. The fame of his teacher would ensure him a supply of students who, unable to study with the great master himself, would be content to earn an *ejazeh* from one of his disciples.

The training of the author of the *Shriaznameh* is a case study in fourteenth-century education, social relations, and kinship. The historian Mowlana Mo'in al-Din Ahmad b. Abu al-Kheir Zarkub (ca. 1300–1387) was also a preacher in the Baghdadi mosque, and, as his title Mowlana suggests, an eminent teacher and scholar. In his work, the *Shiraznameh,* Zarkub provides us his scholarly resume, giving biographies of his teachers, the details of his *ejazehs,* and the works he studied.[45]

His maternal uncle, *Sheikh Haj Rokn al-Din Mansur Baghnovi* (d. 1333). With him Zarkub studied two works on *hadith* (tradition): the *Sahih* of al-Bokhari and the *Masabih al-Sonnat.*[46]

Sheikh Zahir al-Din Abd al-Rahman b. Ali b. Bozghash (d. 1316). In 1313, Zarkub read the sufi work *Awaref al-Ma'aref* with him.[47]

Sheikh Rokn al-Din Yunes b Sadr al-Din b. Shams al-Din Mohammad Safi (d. 1317). Under him Zarkub studied *Kanz al-Khafi min Ikhtiyarat al-Safi,* a sufi work by Rokn al-Din's ancestor, Safi al-Din Osman Kermani (d. ca. 1237).[48]

Mowlana Nur al-Din Mohammad b. Haj Sharaf al-Din Osman Khorasani (d. 1341). In 1320, Zarkub studied *Havi al-Saghir,* an important work of Shafe'i jurisprudence, under Mowlana Mohammad's tutelage.[49]

Qotb al-Din Mohammad Fali-Sirafi (d. 1321), the author of the famous *Sharh-e-Qasideh-ye-Ashknavaniyeh.*[50] With him Zarkub studied Qoranic commentaries and other branches of Islamic scholarship, reading Qotb al-Din's own *Towzih-e-Kashshaf* and the *Miftah al-Ulum* of al-Sakaki (d. 1229).

Taj al-Din Mohammad b. Sharaf al-Din Zanjani (d. 1322 at Delhi). With this teacher Zarkub read two works by the famous Qazi Naser al-Din Abdullah Beiza'i: the *Manhaj* (on methodology, or *osul*) and the *Misbah al-Arwah* on theology.[51]

Amin al-Din Mohammad Baliyani Kazeruni (d. 1344), one of Hafez's "Five Nobles of Fars." Amin al-Din was Zarkub's sufi master, who, in 1317 in Kazeroun, granted the "inspiration of awareness" *(talqin-e-zekr)* to his disciple.[52]

In this manner Zarkub studied the branches of Islamic learning in the seminaries of Shiraz, a city which took great pride in its accomplished teachers. In addition to the branches of learning listed in Zarkub's curriculum vitae, students also studied Qoran-reading *(qara'at),* logic *(manteq),* and Arabic and Persian literature *(adab).* Studying philosophy was frowned upon as irreligious and in opposition to *kalam* (theology). The sources record how one of the most eminent teachers of Shiraz, Mowlana Qavam al-Din Abdullah (d. 1370), flirted with philosophy in his youth. Repenting of this unbelief, he confessed his error to his father-in-law, Sheikh Ja'far Mowsoli, who advised him to "renew his marriage."[53] Studying philosophy had apparently made Qavam al-Din an unbeliever, and thus unqualified to be husband to a Muslim woman.

Every great teacher of Shiraz had his own circle of disciples and associates who would meet regularly for prayer, scholarly discussions, and socializing. One such group centered on the above-mentioned Mowlana Qavam al-Din Abdullah, whose pupils included the poet Hafez and the ruler Shah Shoja.[54] Other, less famous pupils of Qavam al-Din were Zein al-Din Na'ini, Mowlana Najm al-Din Mahmud Kazeruni (preacher in the Khasseh Mosque), and Haji Ali Assar, a wealthy merchant who would supply the poor oil and honey from his shop.[55]

One of Mowlana Qavam al-Din's earliest teachers was Imam Naser al-Din Mohammad b. Mas'ud (d. 1305), who had his own circle of disciples who met weekly for sufi ceremonies at his home in the *sepidan* (or *sepan-dan*) quarter of the Sheikh-e-Kabir district. Attendance at these meetings was limited to twenty-one persons, including Sheikh Zahir al-Din Abd al-Rahman b. Ali b. Bozghash (d. 1316) and Mowlana Jamal al-Din Kuhgiluye'i. Although Imam Naser al-Din never left his house except for Friday prayers, attendance at his circle was considered a privilege and a sign of status. No less a figure than the *qazi al-qozat* of the period, Rokn al-Din Fali-Sirafi (d. 1307), used to call on Imam Naser al-Din every Tuesday.[56]

Najib al-Din Ali b. Bozghash (1198–1279), father of one of Imam Naser al-Din's disciples, also had an impressive group of followers and associates. One of Najib al-Din's students was Qavam al-Din Abdullah's father-in-law, Sheikh Ja'far Mowsoli (d. ca. 1312). Another (would-be) disciple was the famous Sheikh Safi al-Din Ardabili, the ancestor of the Safavid rulers, who traveled to Shiraz for the express purpose of studying with Sheikh Najib al-Din, but arrived just after the scholar's death.[57] In addition to having married the granddaughter of the *naqib* of Fars, Sheikh Najib al-Din was associated with Sheikh Taj al-Din Ahmad Horr, a leading preacher of Shiraz; with Amir Asil al-Din Alavi-Mohammadi (d. 1286); and with Qazi Imam al-Din Omar Beiza'i (d. 1276), the father of the famous chief judge, scholar, and historian.[58]

These teachers attained preeminence through years of study, a proper collection of *ejazeh*s, and, just as important, powerful family connections. The three above-mentioned scholars—Mowlana Qavam al-Din, Imam Naser al-Din, and Najib al-Din Ali—with their retinues of students and associates were all members of important Shirazi families.[59] Another group of outstanding Shirazi teachers in the late thirteenth century consisted of three aristocrats who had studied in the *rabat* of Sheikh-e-Kabir with the famous Shafe'i teacher and sufi master, Sheikh Mo'in al-Din Abdullah b.

Joneid b. Ruzbeh Kathki (d. 1253). The three were Sa'en al-Din Hosein Salmani, Sadr al-Din Mozaffar Baghnovi, and Amir Seyyed Asil al-Din Abdullah Alavi-Mohammadi.[60]

Membership in an aristocratic family was not the only qualification for education and advancement, but it gave young students the advantage of access to Shiraz's most eminent teachers, who might be blood relatives, relatives by marriage, or otherwise associated with a student's powerful family members. Such a network of friendships and relationships meant that the young aristocrat would have a much easier time securing *ejazeh*s than would someone lacking connections to the leading Shirazi families.

Outsiders did attain high positions in Shiraz's scholarly heirarchy, but that achievement usually took extraordinary efforts and patronage from a powerful local figure. When Sheikh Ja'far Mowsoli, the father-in-law of Qavam al-Din Abdullah, first came to Shiraz, he remained unknown, frequenting religious gatherings and remaining silent. People considered him a common, ordinary man until Sheikh Najib al-Din Ali recognized him as an authority. Only then, and with Sheikh Najib al-Din's blessing, did Sheikh Ja'far establish a reputation for learning among the Shirazis.[61]

Early in the seventh/thirteenth century, when Qazi Jamal al-Din Abu Bakr Mesri first came to Shiraz, he found that no one in the city paid attention to him and that he was unable to earn a living. Facing poverty, he made himself a suit of paper clothes and sat in the vestibule of the school where Amid al-Din Afzari, the Atabek's minister, was teaching. When the minister asked the meaning of his clothes, Jamal al-Din answered:

> In Egypt it is the custom that anyone who has suffered injustice puts on paper clothes as a sign of protest. I, a learned man, have come to this city seeking advancement; but things are so bad here that I have had to sell my books.[62]

In this way, Jamal al-Din received official patronage and eventually rose to become chief judge of Fars.

A century later, the custom of wearing paper clothes to protest injustice must have become familiar in Shiraz. Hafez, complaining of the injustice of a patron's leaving Shiraz without telling him, wrote:

یاد باد آنکه ز ما وقت سفر یاد نکرد   به وداعی دل غمدیده ما شاد نکرد

کاغذین جامه بخونابه بشویم که فلک   ره نمونیم به پای علم داد نکرد

Recall that one who forgot us at the time of departure,
Who did not ease our grieving heart with a farewell.
I will wash my paper clothes with bloody tears,
Because heaven did not lead us to the flag of justice.

Sufi Masters and Disciples: Passing the Kherqeh

Sufism arose from the Muslim believer's desire for a religious experience more personal than what strict orthodoxy could offer. The believer, who still observed the tenets of orthodoxy, traveled the sufi path *(tariqat)* and attained this personal religious experience by asceticism, prayer, group ritual, and the understanding of esoteric knowledge *(erfan)*—all under the guidance of a sufi master, called *pir* or *sheikh*.[63]

In the fourteenth century sufism permeated all aspects of life in Shiraz. The poems of Hafez are full of images from sufi belief and practice, the meanings of which in many instances are still obscure.[64] Even Sheikh *At'ameh* (d. 1436), the Shirazi poet of food, gives his recipe for *bu-ard* in the vocabulary of sufi practices familiar to his readers:

> *Bu-ard* is a kind of disciple *(morid)* that the master *(morshed)* in his patched-cloak *(zhendehpush),* which is vinegar, orders to retreat to its cell (the vat) for forty days of fasting and prayer *(chelleh).* There he will experience revelation *(mokashefat)* from the world of molasses. Then he will come to the sufi retreat *(khaneqah)* of the table and sit at the prayer-carpet of bread with the other followers *(moridan),* who are the herbs. There in the world of esoteric knowledge *(erfan),* he should recite the following verse:

هجر کشیدیم تا بوصل رسیدیم   آیه رحمت پس از عذاب نویسند

We endured separation to reach union.
For they write the verse of mercy after punishment.[65]

By tradition, during the Buyid period Mohammad b. Khafif (882–982), famous as Sheikh-e-Kabir, first brought sufism to Shiraz.[66] In this saint's own statement of beliefs, he presents the doctrines of the sufis as follows:

> The sufi believes that poverty is more excellent than riches and that total abstinence is better than abstinence in part. . . . Freedom from the bondage of servanthood is absurd, but freedom from the bondage of carnal desire is possible. . . . Human attributes in gnostics pass away, in neophytes abate. . . . Spiritual intoxication is right for neophytes, but wrong for gnostics.[67]

Many sufi teachings came to Shiraz from Baghdad in the sixth/twelfth century. In the first half of that century, Sheikh Qotb al-Din Abdullah Ali b. Hosein Makki, whom the Shirazis called Sheikh al-Eslam, studied with the two great rival sufi masters of Iraq, Abd al-Qader Gilani and Ibn Rafa'i (Ahmad Kabir). Returning to Shiraz, Sheikh Qotb al-Din introduced sufi ideas into his preaching. Near the the end of the century, another great teacher of Shiraz, Sheikh Mo'in al-Din Abdullah Kathki (d. 1253), studied sufism in Baghdad with Zia al-Din b. Sakineh, one of the greatest masters of the period. Kathki in turn became teacher to three of the leading scholars of late thirteenth-century Shiraz.[68]

The overwhelming predominance of the Shafe'i law school in Shiraz meant that sufism there did not conflict with orthodoxy, and the great Shirazi teachers and scholars could be followers of both *shari'at* (Islamic law) and *tariqat* (the sufi path).[69] Just as the Shirazis measured a scholar's learning in *olum* (Islamic learning) by the quality of his *ejazehs*, they weighed his credentials in *tasawwof* (sufism) by his *selseleh,* or the chain of sufi masters who had invested him with the *kherqeh* (Persian *zhendeh*), the patched cloak of the dervishes.

The *kherqeh* was the uniform of the sufi, a symbol of his service to God through obedience to his *morshed,* or master. He received it from the *morshed* when he was judged ready for initiation. There existed a detailed set of etiquette and beliefs concerning receiving and wearing the *kherqeh,* and about its condition and color.[70] In putting on the *kherqeh,* the wearer, by changing his outward appearance, gave up his previous (sinful) habits and desires. The cloak was ultimately a symbol of holy poverty worn in imitation of the first Moslems. Wearing the *kherqeh,* however, left the wearer open to charges of hypocrisy and ostentatious display of poverty and piety.

Hafez's poems contain many references to wearing the *kherqeh*, not all of which are complimentary.[71] In one verse he says:

خرقه پوشی من از غایت دینداری نیست   پرده ای بر سر صد عیب نهان میپوشم

My wearing the dervish-cloak is not because of piety.
It is a cover that I wear over a hundred hidden faults.

In Shiraz the relationship between bestower and receiver of the *kherqeh* created a network which reinforced ties among family members and between students and teachers. A person's status in the social, religious, and academic hierarchy of the city came from his family connections, the quality and quantity of his scholarly diplomas (*ejazehs*), and his chain of sufi masters *(selseleh)*. In the earliest period, the social status of one's sufi master was less important. For example, the *Shiraznameh* records that the great Ibn Khafif received his *kherqeh* from a Sheikh Ja'far, who was only a shoemaker.[72]

By the sixth/twelfth century, however, sufism was becoming mixed with family connections and status. The great Sheikh Ruzbehan Baqli (1128–1210) settled in the Bagh-e-Now quarter of Shiraz to be near one of his earliest sufi masters, Sheikh Abu Bakr b. Omar Barkâr (d. 1145), a person of no social eminence. Later, Ruzbehan received a *kherqeh* from Sheikh Saraj al-Din Mahmud b. Salbeh (d. 1167), a member of the prestigious family of the sheikhs of Beiza.[73]

By the thirteenth and fourteenth centuries the aristocrats of Shiraz were exchanging sufi credentials among themselves. Joneid Shirazi (d. 1391, the author of *Shadd al-Izar,* received his *kherqeh* from his paternal great-uncle, Sheikh Zia al-Din Abd al-Vahab b. Mozaffar Baghnovi (d. 1342). Ahmad Zarkub, author of the *Shiraznameh,* received his *kherqeh* from his maternal uncle, Sheikh Rokn al-Din Mansur Baghnovi (d. 1333), who had in turn received his from Sheikh Yusef Sarvestani (d. 1283).[74] Zarkub's ancestor, Sheikh Ezz al-Din Mowdud (d. 1265), gave a *kherqeh* to Seyyed Taj al-Din Ja'far Musavi (1217–1304), the *naqib* of Fars. Taj al-Din's son and the next *naqib,* Seyyed Ezz al-Din Ahmad b. Ja'far Musavi (d. 1313), received his *kherqeh* from Sheikh Najib al-Din Ali b. Bozghash. Sheikh

Najib al-Din, whom we have earlier noted as an eminent teacher, received both an *ejazeh* and his *kherqeh* from Sheikh Shahab al-Din Omar Sohravardi (d. 1235), a member of a family of famous sufi masters of Baghdad. Sohravardi himself (see footnote 47 in this chapter) traced his sufi *selseleh* to Sheikh-e-Kabir.[75]

For the most part these sufi masters were not persons withdrawn from the world. As members of the most powerful and wealthy families of Shiraz, they consorted with rulers and ministers and controlled great wealth in the endowments of the dervish lodges *(khaneqah).*[76] Although sufism, like education, was theoretically open to all, its leading practitioners in fourteenth-century Shiraz were members of the great families. One exception noted in the sources was Sheikh Shams al-Din Mohammed Sadeq (d. 1336), who, after miraculously becoming learned, traveled to Kazeroun and received his *kherqeh* from Sheikh Amin al-Din Baliyani.[77]

This upper-class bias may have prevented sufism in Shiraz from becoming a social or political movement, like that of the Sarbedarids in Khorasan or the later Safavid leaders of Ardabil. The sufi masters of Shiraz, like the chief judge and the leader of the *seyyeds*, were solid members of the establishment, if not of the ruling elite. With the support of the rulers, they could strengthen their own financial position and obtain valuable tax exemptions for the *khaneqah*. With the interests of the sufi orders linked to those of the patricians, we would have to look elsewhere to find a base for social movements among the Shirazis.

ARTS AND LETTERS

The rich cultural life of Shiraz in the age of Hafez occurred in spite of (or perhaps because of) the political instability of this period.[78] During the fourteenth century, Shiraz, although torn by internal and external violence, remained a center of painting, religious scholarship, and some of the world's greatest poetry. During this period, Shiraz, along with Tabriz, was one of the major centers of book illustration in Iran. In Tabriz the influence of Chinese painting was very strong, but in Shiraz, farther from the Mongol court, a more traditional Iranian style of painting survived. Four illuminated *Shahnameh* manuscripts have survived from the Inju period in Shiraz. All are dated between 1330 and 1352. One manuscript, dated 1341, was dedicated to Qavam al-Din Hasan, Abu Eshaq's great minister and patron of the arts.[79]

Islamic Scholarship

Shiraz earned its name *Dar al-Elm,* above of learning, from the presence of so many famous teachers and scholars. In Hafez's time, these scholars produced some original work and numerous commentaries *(sharh)* upon older works, or commentaries upon commentaries *(hashiyeh).* Near the end of Hafez's lifetime, the most outstanding scholar of Shiraz was Mir Seyyed Sharif Alameh Jorjani (1339–1413). Mir Seyyed Sharif was first brought to Shiraz by Shah Shoja in 1377 and was appointed chief instructor *(modarres)* of the Dar al-Shafa Seminary.[80] In 1387, Amir Timur took him to Samarqand, where he remained until the conqueror's death in 1405. Returning to Shiraz, he taught there until his death and was buried in an area south of the Jame' Atiq still known as Dar al-Shafa.[81]

Jorjani's descendants were known in Shiraz as the Sharifi Seyyeds, and were trustees of the endowment of the shrine of Shah-e-Cheragh.[82] Seyyed Sharif wrote mostly in Arabic, his most famous work being the *Ta'rifat,* a dictionary of terms used in sufism. He also composed numerous commentaries, including one on the famous *Kashshaf* of Zamakshari and others on the works of Qazi Majd al-Din Esma'il and Qazi Borhan al-Din Osman Kuhgiluye'i, two of the great chief justices of Fars during Hafez's lifetime. These scholars in turn had composed commentaries on earlier works of jurisprudence, methodology, and sufism.[83]

Jorjani also composed commentaries on the works of the renowned Shirazi scholar and judge, Mowlana Qazi Azod al-Din Abd al-Rahman Iji (d. 1355). Qazi Azod al-Din was an advisor of Shah Sheikh Abu Eshaq Inju, a teacher of Shah Shoja, and one of Hafez's "five notables" of Fars. Azod al-Din's most famous work was the *Mawaqif fi Ilm al-Kalam,* a study of theology, which he dedicated first to Sultan Abu Sa'id's *vazir,* Khwajeh Ghiyath al-Din Rashidi, and then to Shah Sheikh Abu Eshaq. Azod al-Din also composed a work on logic and commentaries on Ibn Hajeb's *Mokhtasar* on methodology.[84]

Poetry

Among Shiraz's artistic achievements in the fourteenth century, poetry was the crown jewel, and the poet Hafez, whose verses we have quoted frequently, was by far the most brilliant figure of this age.[85] But his great-ness should not obscure the existence of other first-rate poets at Shiraz who produced their own masterpieces.[86]

Khwaju Kermani (1280–1352) was born a generations before Hafez and much of his work with the *ghazal,* or lyric, anticipates Hafez's bring-ing that form to perfection. Khwaju was a disciple *(morid)* of Sheikh Amin al-Din Baliyani Kazeruni and traced his sufi line back to Sheikh Mor-shed, whom he eulogized in his poetry. Khwaju also wrote poems in praise of the great men of his age, including Abu Eshaq Inju, his brother Mas'ud Shah, the Mozaffarid minister and judge Borhan al-Din (d. 1359), and Qazi Majd al-Din Esma'il Fali, the great chief judge of Fars.

Hafez modified some of Khaju's verses, and transformed them from the graceful into the beautiful. For example, Khaju says:

منزل ار یار قرین است چه دوزخ چه بهشت   سجده گر به نیاز است چه مسجد چه کنشت

If one is near the beloved, what difference if he be in heaven
    or hell?
If prayer is out of need, what difference if it be in mosque
    or synagogue?

Hafez transformed this verse into:

همه کس طالب یارند چه هشیار و چه مست   همه جا خانهٔ عشق است چه مسجد چه کنشت

Everyone, whether he be drunk or sober, seeks the beloved.
Every place, whether it be mosque or synagogue, is the house
    of love.

Obeid Zakani (d. 1370) was the most original and unusual literary figure of the age. Although most famous as a satirist, Obeid possessed an excel-lent classical education and composed beautiful, serious poems. After com-pleting his studies at Shiraz, he became a judge and teacher at Qazvin, his native town. By his own tongue-in-cheek account, he became a satirist after he saw that other literary pursuits led only to poverty. He relates that he had composed a treatise on rhetoric, which he attempted to present to the king. When the courtiers told him the king was not interested in such garbage, Obeid composed a brilliant panegyric, but the courtiers told him the king did not appreciate the exaggerated flattery of poets. Realizing he would never make a living by serious literature, he began telling coarse jokes and reciting obscene verses. This new policy worked so well that Obeid soon became one of the leading figures at the royal court. When a friend asked how, with all of his learning, Obeid could bear to become a court jester, the poet answered:

ای خواجه مکن تا توانی طلب علم   کاندر طلب راتب هر روزه بمانی

رو مسخرگی پیشه کن و مطربی آموز   تا داد خود از کهتر و مهتر بستانی

O sir, avoid learning as much as you can,
Lest you should always be seeking your daily bread.
Go and be a clown and musician,
So you may earn your living from great and small.[87]

Obeid's satirical works included a collection of jokes (mostly obscene) called *Resaleh-ye-Delgosha;* a satirical essay on the decadent morals of his age, called *Akhlaq al-Ashraf (The Ethics of the Aristocracy);* and the humorous fable *Mush o Gorbeh (Cats and Mice)* containing the famous line which has become a proverb in Persian:

مژدگانی که گربه تائب شد   عابد و زاهد و مسلمانا

Good news! The cat has repented
And become a worshipper, an ascetic, a true Moslem.[88]

Obeid's serious poems included eulogies to famous persons of his era, such as Shah Abu Eshaq Inju, Sultan Oveis Jalayeri, and Shah Shoja Mozaffari.[89] He must have been a member of Shah Abu Eshaq's poets' circle, along with the older Khaju and the younger Hafez. He lived most of his life at Shiraz and wrote verses that showed how he preferred his adopted home to his native Qazvin. Some of his lyrics are quite lovely, including one which begins:

جفا مکن که جفا رسم دلربائی نیست   جدا مشو که مرا طاقت جدائی نیست

Be not false, for that is not the custom of loveliness.
Do not leave, for I cannot bear separation.

According to Arberry, the *ghazals* of Obeid, like those of Khaju, "reveal the author bridging the gap between Sa'di and Hafez." Such a description, however, does not do justice to these poems' beauty and originality.

Joneid Shirazi (d. ca. 800/1398), a member of the patrician Baghnovi family, was not only author of the Arabic biographical dictionary *Shadd al-Izar,* but also a poet, whose *divan* has been collected and edited by the twentieth-century scholar Sa'id Nafisi. Although as a poet he ranks below Khaju and Obeid, his verses contain a simple and charming expression of the sufi ideas that influenced his life and the lives of so many Shirazis. For example:

حدیث عشق تو با کس نمیتوان گفتن   که سر دوست نشاید باین و آن گفتن

ز روی زرد من احوال درد من پیداست   چو روشنست چه حاجت که هر زمان گفتن

خوشا غمی که توان گفت پیش همدردی   مرا غمیست که با کس نمی توان گفتن

No one can be told the story of your love,
For one should not tell a friend's secret to this or that person.
My pain is evident from my pale, jaundiced face.
Since the pain is clear, why say it all the time?
Easy is that sorrow which can be told to a sympathizer;
My sorrow is one that can be told to no one.

7

A Very Special Place

دی وعده داد وصلم و در سر شراب داشت
امروز تا چه گوید و بازش چه در سر است

شیراز و آب رکنی و این باد خوش نسیم
عیبش مکن که خال رخ هفت کشور است

Yesterday he promised to be with me, and the wine was in his brain.
Today what will he say, and what will be in his head?
Shiraz, and the water of Roknabad, and this pleasant breeze
Do not fault it, for it is the beauty spot of seven lands.

—*Hafez*

Shiraz has always been a special place, whether for its magnificent poetry, its saints, its scholars, or its wine. Of course, the traveler who visits Shiraz today will not find a city resembling the one where Hafez lived, studied, and composed his lyrics. The site is the same, but the physical setting and the social and cultural life have changed radically. The city wall, the gates, and most of the old neighborhoods are gone; the *madrasehs* have been replaced by a modern university which, until the revolution of 1979, offered much of its instruction in English. Most of the hundreds of shrines and mosques that once adorned Hafez's "tower of saints" have either disappeared or lie forgotten in some obscure corner of the city, visited only by antiquarians.

What kind of city was Hafez's Shiraz? First, it was an unstable and violent place, where squabbling, self-destructive drunkards and bloodthirsty hypocrites often ruled, and where the inhabitants saw natural disasters, sieges, invasions, street fighting, marauding tribes, and arbitrary and ruinous taxation constantly threatening their precarious security and prosperity. Second, it was a "tower of saints" *(borj al-owliya)*, where holy men spent their lives praying and fasting, and devoted their wealth to helping the poor. Third, it was a city of the *rendan,* full of hedonism and debauchery of every description, where the brothels, the wine shops, and the opium dens did booming business and filled the ruler's treasury with taxes on the proceeds. Fourth, it was an "abode of knowledge *(dar al-elm),* where scholars taught and studied all branches of Islamic learning. Finally, it was a brilliant center of Persian culture, producing superb miniature paintings, calligraphy, and an amazing amount of immortal poetry in a few decades.

How could one city of about 60,000 create such varied perceptions of society and such a rich culture? One reason was Shiraz's good fortune in escaping the worst effects of the Mongol invasions and misrule in the thirteenth and early fourteenth centuries. Timely diplomacy and the city's remoteness from the Mongols' invasion routes and from their power centers in Azarbaijan protected it from much of the devastation that occurred in northern Iran. At the same time, Shiraz could be a sanctuary for artists, scholars, and poets fleeing the insecurity of other areas. Another reason was the rivalry of Shiraz with other dynastic capitals, such as Herat and Baghdad, in the fourteenth century. This rivalry was a stimulus to cultural life, since a poet or scholar unsuccessful at one court could seek his fortune at another. Even within the Mozaffarid realm, the squabbling princes of the family set up rival courts in the provincial towns of Esfahan, Yazd, and Kerman. Still another reason for this flowering was the temper of the rulers themselves. Shah Sheikh Abu Eshaq Inju, for example, considered himself a Sassanian Shahanshah, and as such encouraged the presence of first-class poets and artists at his court. Although vanity played a large role in the rulers' patronage of culture in this period, the sources reveal that many of them, such as Abu Eshaq, Shah Shoja, and Shah Mansur, had a genuine appreciation of Iranian art and poetry.

But how could one city be all the things we have described—a combination of Athens, Dodge City, the Vatican, and Sodom and Gomorrah—and not break apart under the strain? The answer lay in the social structure of Shiraz, which produced a network of relationships and dependencies among the ruling elite, the aristocrats, and the common people. Three kinds of overlapping relationships—of family, of teacher and student, and of sufi master and disciple—strengthened the cohesion of the upper classes. For if the members of the ruling elite—the chief justices and the *naqibs*— only rarely intermarried with the local aristocrats, they also established close relations with the rest of society through the institutions of the *madraseh* and *khaneqah,* which were, in theory at least, open to all.

Although historians and biographers have carefully documented the relationships among the aristocrats of Shiraz, they tell us little about the role of the lower classes in the city's social pattern. What kept them from rebelling against the aristocracy and tearing the city apart? The history of Shiraz in this period suggests that the lower classes did in fact feel that they were a part of city life. Two factors probably account for this attachment: the influence of the *kaluviyan,* who had ties with almost all groups in the city, from the ruler's court to the *pahlevanan* of the neighborhoods and bazaars; and sufism, which offered the possibility of a personal, direct religious experience that did not require years of study or special connections with the aristocracy. Although the Shirazi patricians ran the sufi movements during the thirteenth and fourteenth centuries, these movements remained accessible to people of all classes, who, according to the sources, participated enthusiastically in sufi devotions and ceremonies.

Another feature of Shiraz's history during this period is the stability and continuity of its leading families. Such was not the case in northern Iran. The drastic changes that occurred there during the thirteenth and fourteenth centuries—the catastrophic invasions, the destruction of urban life, the decline of agriculture in favor of nomadic pastoralism, and the addition of a large Turkish element to the population—all meant that the society of the North in the fourteenth century was very different from what had existed before the arrival of the Mongols.

But these events barely touched the urban society of Shiraz. City life, supported by the trade and agriculture of Fars, continued largely unchanged. Turkish and Mongol influence remained limited to the ruling house and the military aristocracy, which had already been Turkish since the eleventh century. Other Turkish immigrants came in relatively small numbers and were soon assimilated into the local population. Most important, the judges, teachers, and sufi masters of the city continued to be drawn from the same aristocratic families, some of which traced their origins to Buyid or even to pre-Islamic times. Most of the leading figures of Shiraz in Hafez's lifetime were members of families that had been important in the city since the sixth/twelfth century, and in some cases even earlier. Families such as Baghnovi, Ruzbehan, Fali-Sirafi, Mosalahi-Beiza'i, and others were able to preserve their wealth and prestige in Shiraz through the chaos of the thirteenth and fourteenth centuries, while violence elsewhere was wiping out entire families and displacing the native Iranian aristocracy.

One last question remains unanswered: How did Shiraz, that bastion of orthodoxy throughout the fourteenth century, come to accept Shi'ism, beginning in the reign of Shah Esma'il Safavi in the sixteenth century? The sources barely mention any role for Shi'ism in the religious life of Shiraz a hundred years before the coming of Shah Esma'il. Although many questions surround the status of Shi'ism, three assertions can be made about it and orthodoxy in pre-Safavid Shiraz. First, members of the upper classes of the city—the judges, teachers, sufi leaders, and *seyyeds*—were overwhelmingly Sunnis of the Shafe'i school and were adamantly opposed to Shi'ism. Second, Shi'ism did exist in fourteenth-century Shiraz, but most likely as a weak movement among the lower classes of the city, who responded to its *ma'rakehs* (popular street shows) and its messianic message. Third, the existence of four shrines at the tombs of relatives of Shia Imams in Shiraz is no evidence for the strength of Shia beliefs in the city. Three of these four shrines were built under the patronage of Sunni rulers and all were held in great reverence by the Sunni population and rulers.[1] Even the ultra-orthodox ruler Mohammad Mozaffar, who had threatened to destroy the poet Sa'di's grave for his "unislamic" poetry, never interfered with the flourishing veneration of these sites.

The adoption of Shi'ism in Shiraz could have been accomplished in one of two ways. First, something could have occurred during the fifteenth century to weaken the hold of orthodoxy over Shiraz and thus ease the adoption of Shi'ism under the Safavids. Or, the adoption of Shi'ism imposed by Shah Esma'il Safavi in the early sixteenth century could have been only superficial at first, with the real conversion of most Iranians to Shi'ism occurring much later.[2] Although the second explanation seems a reasonable one, it remains only a hypothesis.

One final point. This work has studied one city in one period. It has been neither a study of "an Islamic city" nor "the Islamic city." It has been based on the premise that a city which could produce a poet of Hafez's stature in a time of great political instability deserves study on its own merits. Many similarities existed among the cities of Islamic Iran at given periods, and one can generalize about the presence and organization of bazaars, quarters, mosques, schools, sufis, judges, and the like. But when Iranian historians wrote of the unique "temperament" of Shiraz, they understood that something in that city's history had created a special form of urban life there, with a society and culture not duplicated elsewhere.

Hafez himself knew that Shiraz was special, and that whatever was special about it both inspired its poets and spread its fame to the boundaries of the known world. Hafez sang of the link between the city, his verses, and the most distant parts of the Islamic world in his beautiful verses:

خدایا منعم گردان به درویشی و خرسندی   در این بازار اگر سودی است با درویش خرسند است

سیه چشمان کشمیری و ترکان سمرقندی   به شعر حافظ شیراز می رقصند و می نازند

If there is profit in this market, it comes to the contented
    dervish.
Bless me, Lord, with both poverty and contentment.
They boast of and dance to the verses of Hafez of Shiraz—
The dark-eyed beauties of Kashmir and the fair Turks of
    Samarqand.

APPENDIX

THE FIRST FAMILIES OF SHIRAZ

An important feature of Shirazi society was the continuity and stability of its leading families. In other regions of Iran the destruction and turmoil that accompanied the Mongol invasions of the thirteenth century—and their chaotic aftermath—wiped out many ancient aristocratic families. In Shiraz, however, most of the leading families preserved their wealth and influence through the thirteenth and fourteenth centuries despite recurrent, violent political changes. Such social stability in a violent age testifies both to the adaptability of the Shirazi aristocrats (who could retain their influence through frequent changes of ruler) and to the foresight of the rulers themselves, who, whatever their faults, could see the benefit of keeping the local aristocracy and social structure intact.

The genealogies in this section reveal both the continuity of the leading Shirazi families and the network of their relationships, at least among the men of these families. The sources provide very little information about the female side, saying only, "He married a daughter of so-and-so," or "He studied with so-and-so, his maternal uncle." Female names occur only in those rare instances where the woman herself ranked among the saints or scholars. Even among the males, the available sources do not always spell out exact family relationships.[1] The order of a person's *nasab* may vary according to the source used, and there is often confusion over the exact form of names—for example, Mahmud in one source may be Mohammad in another. A *nasab* sometimes refers to an individual's father, sometimes to a more distant ancestor.[2]

The genealogies of three aristocratic clans, each representing a different kind of noble family in fourteenth century Shiraz, are worth considering in detail. The Baghnovis were most famous as preachers and sufi masters, with an extensive, well-documented network of marriage relationships with other aristocratic families of Shiraz. The Fali-Sirafis were best known as teachers and judges, who held a position so lofty that they did not marry into the local nobility. The Alavi-Mohammadis were prestigious local *seyyed*s, who intermarried mostly with other families of Alavis.

THE BAGHNOVIS

Because this was the family of the author of *Shadd al-Izar,* we have extensive information about its members. This family claimed Arab origins and traced its ancestry to the Qoreish tribe and to Omar, the second caliph. It held charters from the Omayyad caliph Omar b. Abd al-Aziz and from the Buyid ruler Azod al-Dowleh. Originally landowners in Fasa, the first of the family to settle in Shiraz was Sheikh Zein al-Din Mozaffar b. Ruzbehan b. Taher, who made his home there during the second half of the twelfth century. Sheikh Mozaffar was most famous as a preacher in the Old Congregational Mosque and in the *rabat* of Sheikh Abu Zare' Ardabili, and as a teacher in the Bagh-e-Now mosque. He associated with the Salghurid Atabek Tekleh b. Mowdud (r. ca. 1175–95) and in his preaching used to tell the rulers, "O Turks, do this and refrain from that!" Although Sheikh Zein al-Din Mozaffar resided in the *Jame' Atiq* area, at his death in 1207 he was buried in the Bagh-e-Now district.[3] It was from this association with the latter area that his descendants took their *nesbat* of Baghnovi.

The true patriarch of the Shiraz Baghnovis, however, was Sheikh Zein al-Din's grandson, Sheikh Sadr al-Din Abu Mo'ali Mozaffar b. Mohammad (d. 1289). Unlike his grandfather, who had traveled widely in Iraq, Arabia, India, and Syria, Sheikh Sadr al-Din spent most of his life in Shiraz, where he studied under the leading teachers of the time, including Qazi Majd al-Din Esma'il Fali, Qazi Jamal al-Din Mesri, Mowlana Emam al-Din Beiza'i, and the sufi leader Sheikh Mo'in al-Din Abdullah Kathki.[4] The ruler, Atabek Abu Bakr, greatly respected him, and offered him his father's post of *va'ez* (preacher) of the Old Congregational Mosque. Sheikh Sadr al-Din, however, refused the appointment, preferring to preach in the smaller, humbler mosque of Bagh-e-Now.

Sheikh Sadr al-Din Mozaffar was most famous as a scholar and a preacher. He also acquired sufi connections by marrying a descendant of the Sheikh al-Shoyukh, Abu al-Hosein Ahmad b. Salbeh Beiza'i (d. 1023), a famous sufi master.[5] The descendants of Sheikh Sadr al-Din, perhaps as a result of this marriage, were deeply involved in sufism in the late thirteenth and the fourteenth centuries.[6]

Sheikh Sadr al-Din Mozaffar had seven sons, all of whom became scholars, and many daughters, who married into important Shirazi families. One of his daughters married Sheikh Shahab al-Din Abu al-Kheir Zarkub, the father of Mo'in al-Din Ahmad, the author of the *Shiraznameh*. One of Sheikh Mo'in al-Din's first teachers was his mother's brother, Sheikh Haj Rokn al-Din Mansur Rastgu, a son of Sheikh Sadr al-Din Mozaffar. Another daughter married into the family of Kasa'i, about which little is known, except that they, like the Zarkubs, were associated with the Baghdadi mosque.[7]

Sheikh Sadr al-Din's eldest son, Sheikh Sa'd al-Din As'ad, died young (1271), before his father. Sheikh Sa'd al-Din's great-grandson was Sheikh Mo'in al-Din Joneid (d. ca. 800/1398), the poet and author of *Shadd al-Izar*. Two of Sheikh Sadr al-Din's sons, Zein al-Din Taher and Rokn al-Din Mansur, married into the families of their father's fellow students: the former married a granddaughter of Faqih Sa'en al-Din Hosein Salmani, author of *Tarikh-e-Mashayekh-e-Fars;* the latter (and more famous son) married a daughter of Amir Asil al-Din Alavi-Mohammadi.[8] The Baghnovis and the Salmanis strengthened their alliance when a grandson of Sheikh Sadr al-Din, Sheikh Taj al-Din Mo'ayyed b. Omar b. Mozaffar, married a great-granddaughter of Faqih Sa'en al-Din.[9]

In addition to their fame as sheikhs and scholars, the Baghnovi family members were always associated with Shiraz's Old Congregational Mosque. Although Sheikh Sadr al-Din had refused to accept the Atabek's invitation to preach there, both his son Haj Rokn al-Din Mansur and his grandson Rokn al-Din Yahya b. Mansur held the post of *va'ez* in that mosque. Shah Sheikh Abu Eshaq also appointed the latter *khatib* (reader of the main Friday address) of that great mosque.[10]

THE FALI-SIRAFIS

Although there are many biographies of this family of Shafe'i judges, we know less about them than we do about the Baghnovis and their associates. Information is sketchier because the sources do not record the marriage ties of the Fali-Sirafis, and the family members' exalted rank as chief judges of Fars kept them above forming marriage alliances with local aristocratic families such as Baghnovi, Ruzbehan, or Zarkub. Judging by their titles of *mowlana* and *qazi,* the Fali-Sirafis were better know as judges and teachers, and presumably less involved in sufism and preaching.

The first member of the family of whom we know more than a name is Qazi Saraj al-Din Abu al-Ezz Mokarram b. Ala Fali (d. 1224), who was chief judge of Fars and khatib of the New Mosque (Masjed-e-Now) in Shiraz.[11] Another chief judge from this family was Qazi Majd al-Din Esma'il (d. 1267), chief judge of Fars for forty years under the Salghurid Atabek Abu Bakr b. Sa'd.[12] Beginning with this first Qazi Esma'il, members of the Fali-Sirafi family were chief judges for three generations. Qazi Rokn al-Din Yahya (d. 1307), the son of Qazi Esma'il, held office during the turbulent period of Mongol rule in the late seventh/thirteenth century. This Qazi Rokn al-Din was also one of the few eminent religious men of Fars who openly opposed the rule of Shams al-Dowleh, Malek-al-Yahud.[13]

Named after his grandfather, Qazi Rokn al-Din's son, Qazi Majd al-Din Esma'il (1271–1355) was chief judge of Fars under the Injus and the most famous figure of the Fali-Sirafi family. Hafez eulogized him in his poems, and Ibn Battuta reported how the rulers, nobles, and ordinary citizens of Shiraz held him in great respect.[14] When Qazi Majd al-Din became nearly blind in his old age, his nephews, Ala al-Din and Majd al-Din, took care of legal matters for him. With the death of Qazi Majd al-Din in 1355, the chief judgeship of Fars passed out of the family of Fali-Sirafi. Although the family continued to be important (there were still eminent Falis in Shiraz in 1972), under the Mozaffarids it lost the lofty position it had occupied under the Salghurids, Mongols, and Injus.

The sources contain biographies of other members of this family whose relationships to the three chief judges are not clear. The fact that all of the Fali-Sirafis held the title *mowlana* indicates that they were most famous as teachers. One collateral branch of this family included Mowlana Qotb al-Din Mohammad b. Abu al-Kheir Fali (d. 712 or 721/1312 or 1321), who composed a famous commentary *(sharh)* on the work of his ancestor, the Salghurid minister Amid al-Din Vazir Afzari.[15] This same Mowlana Qotb al-Din Fali was in some way descended from the family of Qazi Sharaf al-Din Hoseini (d. 1243), a rich and powerful *seyyed* and chief judge of Fars.[16]

THE ALAVI-MOHAMMADIS

As their genealogy shows, in the thirteenth and fourteenth centuries the Alavi-Mohammadis were less a "family" than a series of alliances through the female side, all related to a single figure—Amir Asil al-Din Abdullah (d. 1286 or 1291). Since the Shirazis usually traced family descent through the male line, strictly speaking the Alavi-Mohammadi family ended with the death of Amir Asil al-Din's son, Naser al-Din Yahya b. Abdullah, in the early fourteenth century. Amir Asil-al-Din, however, was such a towering figure that the biographers of his sister's and daughters' children placed great emphasis on their maternal descent, and considered them members of an extended Alavi-Mohammadi family.

The great central figure of this family, distinguished by its members' strict orthodoxy, was Amir Seyyed Asil al-Din Abdullah b. Ali b. Abu Mahasen b. Sa'd b. Mahdi Alavi-Mohammadi.[17] The Mohammadi in his *nesbat* refers to his descent from Mohammad b. Hanafiyeh, a son of the Caliph Ali by a wife of the Hanifeh tribe. Similarly, other *seyyed*s took the *nesbat* of Hasani or Hoseini according to which son of Ali they traced their ancestry to. As a young man, Amir Asil al-Din studied the standard collections of prophetic traditions *(hadith)* with the greatest scholars of his period. He read the famous *Sahih* of Bokhari with Sheikh Ala al-Din Khojandi (d. 1239), who in turn had read that work with Abu al-Vaqt Sajari-Haravi (1165–1257).[18] He also studied other works of *hadith,* including the *Sonon* of Abu Isa al-Termezi (d. 891), with another of the great hadith scholars *(mohaddeth)* of the early thirteenth century, Abu Hafs Omar Dinavari (d. 1232).

Unlike most scholars of his period, Amir Asil al-Din did not travel, but remained in Shiraz, where he composed works on *hadith,* preached in the Old Congregational Mosque, and worked actively against the Shia.[19] He died in 1286 (or 1291) and was buried in the saddle makers' (*Sarrajan* or *Palangaran*) quarter near the mosque where he preached.[20] His son, Naser al-Din Yahya, died apparently without issue in the early fourteenth century and was buried next to his father.

The female side preserved the Alavi-Mohammadi family name. Asil al-Din's sister married a Hoseini *seyyed,* a certain Seyyed Fakhr al-Din Arabshah Hoseini, ancestor of the great Dashtaki-Shirazi family. Although we have no biography of this Seyyed Fakhr al-Din, his son (or grandson, according to one source), Seyyed Baha al-Din Heidar (d. ca. 1339), was a well-known sufi and a scholar of *tafsir* (commentary) and *hadith,* which he had studied with Amir Asil al-Din, his maternal uncle.[21] Baha al-Din's son, Amir Taj al-Din Mohammad (d. 1363), was a famous and powerful preacher, who spent much of this time reading the Qoran and praying. Taj al-Din's son, Jalal al-Din Yahya, was a preacher, scholar, and historian. He wrote prolifically, composing a work entitled *al-Shaikh wa al-Shabb (The Young and the Old).* Like his ancestor, Amir Jalal al-Din also preached and wrote against the Shia.[22]

In addition to his relationship with the Hoseini *seyyed*s, Amir Asil al-Din, through his daughters, established relations with other great families of Shiraz. One daughter married the famous outspoken preacher of the Baghnovi family, Haj Rokn al-Din Mansur Rastgu (d. 1333). Another daughter married a *seyyed* known as Ahmad Va'ez. Their son, Amir Rokn al-Din (d. 1354), and grandson, Amir Seif al-Din Yusef (d. 1362), were preachers in both the Old Congregational and the Mas'udiyeh Mosques.[23]

Baghnovi Family

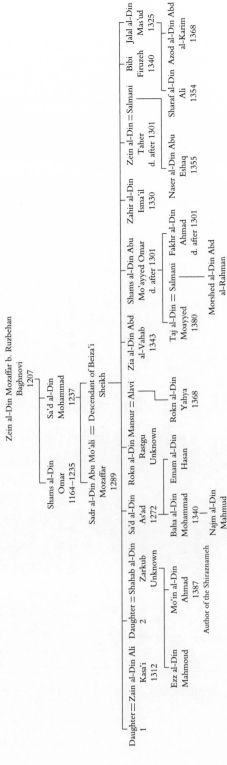

Part of the Fali-Sirafi Family (Qazi al-Qozat of Fars)

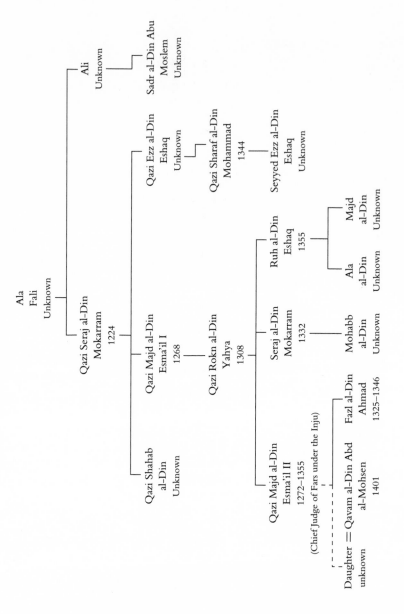

Part of the Fali-Sirafi Family (Chief Judges of Fars)

Amid al-Din Abu Nasr Asad Farsi Afzari
Vazir
1226
(Minister of Atabek Sa'd. Executed by his son,
Atabek Abu Bakr.)

Safi al-Din Abu al-Kheir
Mas'ud
1279

Mowlana Qotb al-Din
Mohammad
1321
(Composed a commentary on the work of
his ancestor, Amid al-Din)

Safi al-Din Abu al-Kheir was related in some way
to Qazi Majd al-Din Esma'il I Fali-Sirafi (d. 1268).

Family Connections of Amir Asil ad-Din Alavi

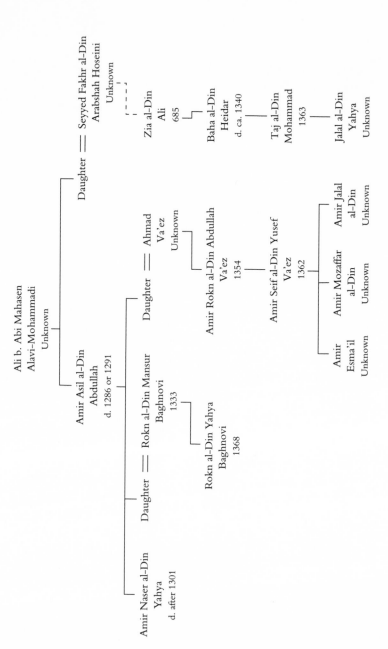

Ali b. Abi Mahasen
Alavi-Mohammadi
Unknown

Amir Asil al-Din
Abdullah
d. 1286 or 1291

Daughter = Seyyed Fakhr al-Din
Arabshah Hoseini
Unknown

Amir Naser al-Din
Yahya
d. after 1301

Daughter = Rokn al-Din Mansur
Baghnovi
1333

Rokn al-Din Yahya
Baghnovi
1368

Daughter = Ahmad
Va'ez
Unknown

Amir Rokn al-Din Abdullah
Va'ez
1354

Amir Seif al-Din Yusef
Va'ez
1362

Amir
Esma'il
Unknown

Amir Mozaffar
al-Din
Unknown

Amir Jalal
al-Din
Unknown

Zia al-Din
Ali
685

Baha al-Din
Heidar
d. ca. 1340

Taj al-Din
Mohammad
1363

Jalal al-Din
Yahya
Unknown

Adib-Salehani Family

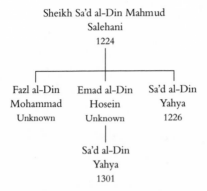

Sheikh Sa'd al-Din Mahmud
Salehani
1224

Fazl al-Din   Emad al-Din   Sa'd al-Din
Mohammad   Hosein   Yahya
Unknown   Unknown   1226

Sa'd al-Din
Yahya
1301

Afzari Family

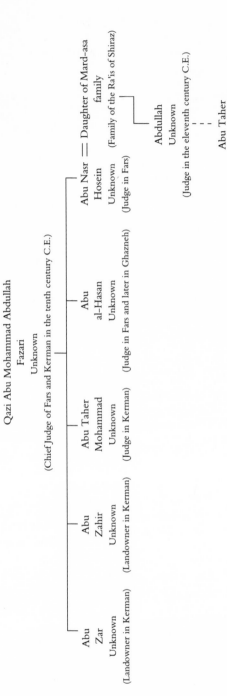

Qazi Abu Mohammad Abdullah
Fazari
Unknown
(Chief Judge of Fars and Kerman in the tenth century C.E.)

Abu Zar — Unknown — (Landowner in Kerman)

Abu Zahir — Unknown — (Landowner in Kerman)

Abu Taher Mohammad — Unknown — (Judge in Kerman)

Abu al-Hasan — Unknown — (Judge in Fars and later in Ghazneh)

Abu Nasr Hosein — Unknown — (Judge in Fars) = Daughter of Mard-asa family (Family of the Ra'is of Shiraz)

Abdullah — Unknown — (Judge in the eleventh century C.E.)

Abu Taher Mohammad — 1099

Qazi Abu Mohammad — Unknown

Arabshah-Hoseini Family

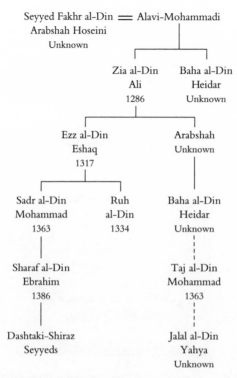

Seyyed Fakhr al-Din ══ Alavi-Mohammadi
Arabshah Hoseini
Unknown

Zia al-Din   Baha al-Din
Ali   Heidar
1286   Unknown

Ezz al-Din   Arabshah
Eshaq   Unknown
1317

Sadr al-Din   Ruh   Baha al-Din
Mohammad   al-Din   Heidar
1363   1334   Unknown

Sharaf al-Din   Taj al-Din
Ebrahim   Mohammad
1386   1363

Dashtaki-Shiraz   Jalal al-Din
Seyyeds   Yahya
                          Unknown

Note: The *Shiraznameh,* 204 lists Arabshah as the son of Zia ad-Din Ali, while *Shadd al-Azar,* says he was the *father* of Zia ad-Din (and Baha ad-Din). The former version corresponds more closely to the dates.

Beiza'i Judges

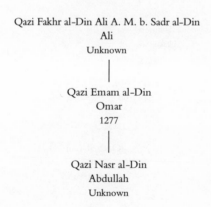

Qazi Fakhr al-Din Ali A. M. b. Sadr al-Din
Ali
Unknown

Qazi Emam al-Din
Omar
1277

Qazi Nasr al-Din
Abdullah
Unknown

Bozghash Family

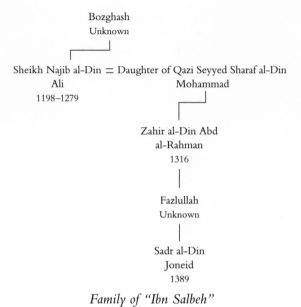

Bozghash
Unknown

Sheikh Najib al-Din = Daughter of Qazi Seyyed Sharaf al-Din
Ali   Mohammad
1198–1279

Zahir al-Din Abd
al-Rahman
1316

Fazlullah
Unknown

Sadr al-Din
Joneid
1389

Family of "Ibn Salbeh"
(Sheikhs of Beiza)

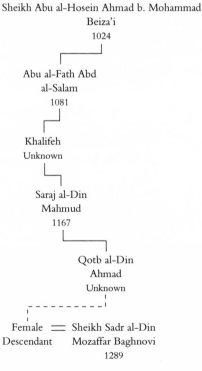

Sheikh Abu al-Hosein Ahmad b. Mohammad
Beiza'i
1024

Abu al-Fath Abd
al-Salam
1081

Khalifeh
Unknown

Saraj al-Din
Mahmud
1167

Qotb al-Din
Ahmad
Unknown

Female   =   Sheikh Sadr al-Din
Descendant   Mozaffar Baghnovi
1289

Mosalahi Beiza'i Family

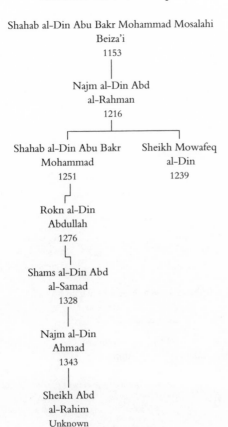

Shahab al-Din Abu Bakr Mohammad Mosalahi
Beiza'i
1153

Najm al-Din Abd
al-Rahman
1216

Shahab al-Din Abu Bakr   Sheikh Mowafeq
Mohammad   al-Din
1251   1239

Rokn al-Din
Abdullah
1276

Shams al-Din Abd
al-Samad
1328

Najm al-Din
Ahmad
1343

Sheikh Abd
al-Rahim
Unknown

Musavi Seyyeds

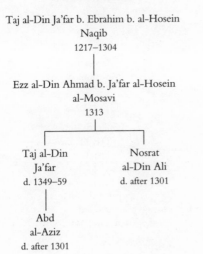

Taj al-Din Ja'far b. Ebrahim b. al-Hosein
Naqib
1217–1304

Ezz al-Din Ahmad b. Ja'far al-Hosein
al-Mosavi
1313

Taj al-Din   Nosrat
Ja'far   al-Din Ali
d. 1349–59   d. after 1301

Abd
al-Aziz
d. after 1301

Ruzbehan and Zarkub Families

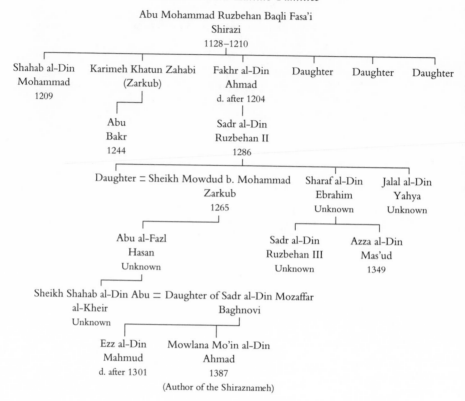

Abu Mohammad Ruzbehan Baqli Fasa'i
Shirazi
1128–1210

Shahab al-Din   Karimeh Khatun Zahabi   Fakhr al-Din   Daughter   Daughter   Daughter
Mohammad   (Zarkub)   Ahmad
1209   d. after 1204

Abu   Sadr al-Din
Bakr   Ruzbehan II
1244   1286

Daughter = Sheikh Mowdud b. Mohammad   Sharaf al-Din   Jalal al-Din
Zarkub   Ebrahim   Yahya
1265   Unknown   Unknown

Abu al-Fazl   Sadr al-Din   Azza al-Din
Hasan   Ruzbehan III   Mas'ud
Unknown   Unknown   1349

Sheikh Shahab al-Din Abu = Daughter of Sadr al-Din Mozaffar
al-Kheir   Baghnovi
Unknown

Ezz al-Din   Mowlana Mo'in al-Din
Mahmud   Ahmad
d. after 1301   1387
(Author of the Shiraznameh)

Family of Ruzbehan Farid

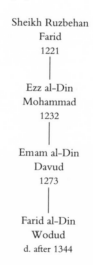

Sheikh Ruzbehan
Farid
1221

Ezz al-Din
Mohammad
1232

Emam al-Din
Davud
1273

Farid al-Din
Wodud
d. after 1344

Salmani Family

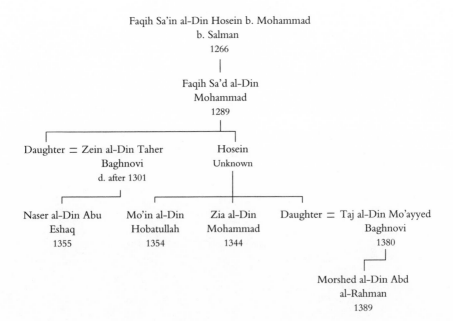

Faqih Sa'in al-Din Hosein b. Mohammad
b. Salman
1266

Faqih Sa'd al-Din
Mohammad
1289

Daughter = Zein al-Din Taher   Hosein
Baghnovi   Unknown
d. after 1301

Naser al-Din Abu   Mo'in al-Din   Zia al-Din   Daughter = Taj al-Din Mo'ayyed
Eshaq   Hobatullah   Mohammad   Baghnovi
1355   1354   1344   1380

Morshed al-Din Abd
al-Rahman
1389

NOTES

1. HISTORY OF SHIRAZ TO THE MONGOL CONQUEST

1. Fars is also nomad country *par excellence*. The proximity of highlands, lowlands, and temperate zones allows nomads, who traditionally produced much of the meat, milk, wool, and carpets of the region, to move relatively short distances between summer and winter pasturage.

2. *Hezar-Mazar,* p. 3.

3. *Nozhat al-Qolub,* p. 112.

4. *Hodud al-Alam,* p. 126.

5. For descriptions of these pre-Islamic remains, see Mostafavi, pp. 77–79, Emdad, pp. 127–28, Frye, *Sassanian Remains,* and Whitcomb, *Before the Roses and Nightingales.*

6. The *Farsnameh* of Ibn al-Balkhi, pp. 130–35, describes the campaigns in detail.

7. On the relationship of Zoroastrianism and Islam in Fars during the first centuries of Islam, see Frye, *Heritage,* pp. 278–91.

8. The sources give no account of the discovery of the grave of Mohammad b. Musa (Mir Mammad to today's Shirazis), the third brother. In Shiraz it matters less *who* is really buried in these graves than who people *think* is buried there. Members of the Alid family did flee from Ma'mun's agents in the early ninth century, and it is quite possible that some took refuge in Shiraz, where they may have died in obscurity or have been discovered and executed. The question of when someone was buried in the vicinity of the Jame' Atiq is also important—that particular area of Shiraz has always been a popular place of burial. The eighth/fourteenth century source *Shadd al-Izar* lists forty-four grave sites in the area. Although the earliest fixed date given for a grave there is 447/1055, other graves were, by reputation and tradition, much older. In 1971, a number of ancient Islamic graves near the Jame' Atiq were still extant. Thus, in the course of clearing land near the mosque, the Atabek's minister could have found an old gravestone, which, by some process, was attributed to Ahmad b. Musa. In other words, a third/ninth century gravestone could certainly have existed in that neighborhood of Shiraz.

9. By 1972, the main bazaar of Shiraz had moved north, and the modest Bazar-e-Haji occupied the site of the old main bazaar.

10. Estakhri, p. 99. *Tassuj* may also mean rural district, and Estakhri may be referring to districts of the Shiraz region rather than to urban quarters. However, the *tassuj* he calls Dastakan may refer to the urban area later known as Dashtak, south of the

Old Congregational Mosque. None of the other districts could be identified as either urban or rural.

11. Engineer M. Pirnia, Office for Preservation of Historical Monuments, Teheran. Personal Communication, 1971.

12. Ali Sami, in *Shiraz: Diyar Sa'di va Hafez*, p. 492, has a photo of the inscription at Abu Zare'.

13. These uprisings were in some way connected to the Isma'ili and Bateni heresies, for the historians report that large numbers of the Shabankareh were Isma'ili. For the history of the Shabankareh, see *Montakhab-e-Tarikhi-ye-Mo'ini*, pp. 1–9, and Setudeh, vol. II, pp. 20–42. By Mongol times, Shabankareh had become the name of the district between Fars and Kerman, known from Sassanian times as Darabgerd Khurreh. It included the towns of Ij (or Ig, near modern Estahbanat), Neyriz, and Darabgerd. The Shabankareh first appeared in the late Buyid era, but the dynast's founders traced their ancestry to the Sassanian period. The dynasty survived until 1355, when the Mozaffarids finally destroyed it.

14. *Farsnameh* of Ibn Balkhi, pp. 133–134.

15. Ayati-Vassaf, pp. 91–92.

16. *Shiraznameh*, p. 73. The site still existed in 1972, but had reverted to its former obscurity in a small room behind the modern Bazar-e-Now.

17. Based on the dates, this could be the grave of Torkan Khatun, sister of Ala al-Dowleh, Atabek of Yazd, and wife of Atabek Sa'd b. Abu Bakr (d. 661/1263) and later of Atabek Salghurshah b. Salghur (r. 1263–64).

18. Ayati-Vassaf, p. 91.

19. *Shadd al-Izar*, p. 325.

20. Atabek Abu Bakr resented the minister's correspondence with Sultan Mohammad Khwarezmshah and his consideration of a post at the Sultan's court. Amid al-Din As'ad apologized in the following verse:

اى وارث تاج و مملكت سعد   بخشاى خداى را به جان و سر سعد

بر من چو خويشتن تا هستم   همچو الف ايستاده ام بر سر سعد

O inheritor of Sa'd's crown and kingdom,
For God's sake pardon me, by the soul of Sa'd.
Straight I will always stand for you,
As I stood like the *alef* at the head of your father's name.

But the Atabek, remembering that As'ad had helped suppress Abu Bakr's revolt against his father in 1217, was unmoved by this neat verse and by the fact that both of their names began with the same letter (*alef*). He had the prisoner executed in 1227. It remained for a descendant, Qazi Qotb al-Din Mohammad Fali (d. ca. 1320), to preserve Amid al-Din's fame by writing a famous exposition on Amid al-Din's work, called *Sharh-e-Ashknavaniyeh*. Ayati-Vassaf, p. 92; *Shadd al-Izar*, p. 433.

2. THINGS FALL APART

1. Ayati-Vassaf, pp. 107–8. They claimed he was unfit to rule and had killed innocent people. His capital offense, however, was ignoring his mother-in-law's advice.

2. The White Fortress *(Qal'eh-ye-Sefid)*, northwest of Kazeroun in the area now called Mamasani, is one of the most famous castles of Fars. It is described in *Farsnameh-ye-Naseri,* vol. II, pp. 334–5, and *Asar-e-Ajam,* p. 302.

3. Many contemporary Iranian historians possess a streak of male chauvinism. See, for example, Enjavi Shirazi, pp. 51–3.

4. Forsat Shirazi in *Asar-e-Ajam,* pp. 579–80, lists twenty-five governors of Fars from the end of effective Salghurid power (about 1267) until Abu Eshaq's taking power in 1343. Thus the average term of office was about three years.

5. An enraged population had driven her opponents out of the city in 1281, and Abesh's return to Shiraz the following year was the occasion for a month's celebration. Ayati-Vassaf, p. 124, and *Shiraznameh,* p. 93.

6. This distinction is not absolute, since Seyyed Emad al-Din, the bitter enemy of the Atabek's party, also had his supporters in Shiraz. Both Zarkub, the author of the *Shiraznameh,* and Vassaf testified to the Seyyed's noble qualities. Nor was the distinction between the two parties an ethnic one, since both groups included persons of Persian, Turkish, and Mongol origin.

7. The Nikudar Mongols, named for their first commander, Nikudar, had been soldiers of the Joshid princes Tutar and Qular, who were allegedly poisoned while accompanying Hulagu Khan on his campaign in Iran ca. 1260. After the death of the two princes, their troops fled to the area of Ghazneh, in present-day Afghanistan (*Cambridge History of Iran,* vol. V, p. 353).

8. Once he questioned Sheikh Najib al-Din Ali b. Bozghash (1197–1279), one of the greatest scholars of Shiraz, on the question of man's rank in the cosmos. Before the sheikh had finished answering, Enkiyanu left the meeting. Later he sent a message of apology, saying, "I realize that my action was impolite, but I feared that if I stayed I would soon abandon the religion of my ancestors." (Ayati-Vassaf, pp. 112–3)

9. This was the mission of Suqunchaq No'in in 1272 and 1279. Also of Seyyed Emad al-Din in 1281 and 1283 and of Jowshi and Shams ad-Dowleh in 1289. *Shiraznameh,* p. 90 ff.

10. Eqbal, in his notes to *Shadd al-Izar,* pp. 543–48, gives an account of this family. Tib was a small town in lower Iraq, near the present-day Iran-Iraq border. Once a minister of the Saheb-Divan (Royal Treasurer) brought Jamal al-Din an order for payment of 100 *toman* (ten million dinars) in gold and 1,500 *man* (about 7,500 pounds) of pearls within ten days. Jamal al-Din, "for the sake of his honor and good name," turned over thirty thousand *toman*s of his personal fortune (Ayati-Vassaf, 162).

11. In 1297, when he had defeated his rival, Ezz al-Din Mozaffar Amid, he was granted "complete unshared authority" over both the land and sea areas of Fars. He was again confirmed in his position by the Royal Treasurer Shams al-Din Mohammad b. Mohammad Joveini in 704/1304 after the accession of Sultan Oljaitu (1304–16). But in 1300, after drought, famine, and cholera the previous year had killed

thousands of people in Fars, Jamal al-Din was unable to prevent the Mongol tax collectors from descending on Shiraz and collecting the full arrears due from the previous two years, including 330,000 dinars from Jamal al-Din himself.

12. An account of the Chupani family, which later became very important in Shiraz, can be found in Ghani, p. 17 ff.

13. The sources for this period include Mahmud Kotbi's *Zeil-e-Tarikh-e-Gozideh*, Zarkub's *Shiraznameh*, Hafez Abru's *Zeil-e-Jame' al-Tavarikh*, and the *Montakhab-e-Tavarikh-e-Mo'ini*. Secondary sources include Eqbal's *Tarikh-e-Moghul*, Ghani's *Tarikh-e-Asr-e-Hafez*, and the nineteenth-century *Farsnameh-ye-Naseri*. In English there is *The Cambridge History of Iran*, vol. V, and E. G. Browne's *Literary History of Persia*, vol. III.

14. Thus, during the last ten years of the reign of Abu Sa'id, Korduchin's rule in Fars must have been only nominal, with real power in the hands of the Inju family— Mahmud Shah and his two elder sons, Mas'ud Shah and Keikhosrow.

15. Hafez Abru, pp. 142–3; Ghani, pp. 6–8; *Farsnameh-ye-Naseri*, vol. I, p. 49. After their release, Mahmud Shah returned to the Mongol court and Mas'ud Shah remained in Asia Minor as the deputy of the governor, Sheikh Hasan-e-Bozorg Ilkani.

16. *The Cambridge History of Iran*, vol. V, pp. 413–17, gives an account of these struggles.

17. The poet has a nice pun here using خایه دار meaning both "brave" (figuratively) and "one who holds testicles" (literally).

18. *Farsnameh-ye-Naseri*, vol. I, p. 53; *Tarikh-e-Moghul*, p. 362; Browne, *The Literary History of Persia*, vol. III, p. 60, and others recount these gruesome events.

19. *Shiraznameh*, p. 105. The *Montakhab-e-Tavarikh-e-Mo'ini*, p. 173, says that Pir Hosein tried to kill Amir Mohammad. But all other sources follow Zarkub, who must have been an eyewitness.

20. *Safarnameh*, pp. 199–200.

21. Although the sources praise Mas'ud Shah as very generous and as the benefactor of many public buildings in Fars, he was not much of a military leader.

22. Zarkub (*Shiraznameh*, p. 106) notes the date of this siege as follows:

چهارشنبه بیست و ششم ز ماه ربیع   به هفتصد و چهل و یک به غر و حشمت و ناز

رسید موکب نوئین عصر پیر حسین   به انتقام دگر بار بر در شیراز

On Wednesday, the twenty-sixth of the month of Rabi'
In the year 741, the forces of Pir Hosein,
The commander of the age, in pomp and splendor,
Returned for revenge to the gates of Shiraz.

23. In these struggles, three members of the Chupani family fought on different sides. United, the Chupanis might have been able to restore (for better or worse) some kind of central authority in Iran. In the case of the Inju, one brother's yielding peaceably to another was out of keeping with the spirit of the times. Abu Eshaq may have felt himself too weak to challenge his elder brother, who still had support from Yaghi

Basti's forces. The Shirazi aristocrats also considered Mas'ud Shah, by reason of age and experience, the legitimate successor to his father.

24. Within a year Malek Ashraf had gained control of the family and had murdered his uncle Yaghi Basti. He continued his brutal reign in Tabriz until 1356.

3. SHIRAZ AS CITY-STATE

1. Amir Pir Hossein Chupani had given rule of Kerman to Amir Mohammad in 1341, after the latter had helped in the recapture of Shiraz. Amir Mobarez al-Din Mohammad b. Mozaffar traced his descent to a certain Ghiyath al-Din Haji of Khwaf in Khorasan, who had migrated to Yazd during the first Mongol attacks on Iran in the 1220s. Ghiyath al-Din's grandson, Amir Sharaf al-Din Mozaffar, served under the Atabeks of Yazd and then under the Mongol Il-Khans. Sultan Khodabandeh-Oljaitu (r. 1303–16) appointed Amir Mozaffar road guardian of central Iran and the ruler of Meibod and Abarqu, both subdistricts of Yazd. After Amir Mozaffar died in 1313, his son Amir Mobarez al-Din Mohammad took his father's position of local ruler and road guardian. His success in defending Yazd against Nikudari bandits and in keeping the roads open in his area earned him support and favor at the Mongol court. In 1336, during the anarchy that followed the death of Sultan Abu Sa'id, Amir Mohammad expelled the Mongol governor of Yazd and took control of that city.

2. Amir Mohammad later noted how he had equipped seventy horsemen from the sale of a jewelled harp he had captured from Abu Eshaq's nephew at Kerman (Kotbi, p. 35).

3. The scholar Azod al-Din Iji (d. 1355) was one of those praised by Hafez in his famous poem "Rejal-e-Mamlakat-e-Fars" ("The Great Men of the Realm of Fars"). Azod al-Din wrote in Arabic, and his most famous work is *Mawaqif fi Ilm al-Kalam (The Stations of Theology)*. During this mission, Amir Mohammad's son Shah Shoja took advantage of the scholar's presence in camp to study one of his works (Kotbi, p. 37).

4. *Farsnameh-ye-Naseri*, vol. I, pp. 54–55. At another time he took a companion onto the roof of his palace to show him the beauties of Shiraz in the spring. Seeing the besieging army outside the city, he asked, "What is that?" When he learned it was Amir Mohammad's army he said with a smile, "What a fool he must be to deprive himself and us of happiness in the delightful spring."

5. Concerning Abu Eshaq's debt to these figures, see above, chapter 2.

6. The traveler Ibn Battuta, visiting Shiraz during Abu Eshaq's rule in 1347, noted that the Shirazis were not allowed to carry arms in the city because of their bravery and rebelliousness (*Safarnameh*, p. 199). The aristocrat historian Zarkub writes (*Shiraznameh*, p. 111):

مثل زنند که صد سال ظلم و جور ملوک   به از دو روزه شر عام و فتنه غوغاست

The proverb says that a century's tyranny and oppression of kings
Is better than two day's anarchy and riot.

7. Hafez mentions Qavam al-Din in five of his poems, including the famous *Rejal-e-Mamlakat-e-Fars*. For example:

دریای اخضر فلك و كشتی هلال ہستند غرق نعمت حاجی قوام ما

The green sea of the heavens and the ship of the crescent moon
Are swamped in the gifts of our Haji Qavam.

and:

برندی شهره شد حافظ میان همدمان لیکن چه غم دارم که در عالم قوام الدین حسن دارم

Hafez is notorious among his companions for *rendi,* but
What do I care, who in this world have Qavam al-Din Hassan?

For more about Haji Qavam al-Din, see Ghani, pp. 144–51.

8. See above, chapter 1. On the history of the Shabankareh dynasty, see *Montakhab-e-Tavarikh-e-Mo'ini,* pp. 1–9, and Setudeh, vol. II, pp. 20–42.

9. Kalu Omar, the chief of Murdestan, hid in a cave, and many of the quarter's inhabitants disguised themselves in women's clothes and took refuge with relatives in the protected Kazeroun Gate neighborhood.

10. In 1354, Amir Mohammad had sworn allegiance to the Abbasid caliph in Egypt and had received the title "Deputy of the Commander of the Faithful." Thus the name of the Abbasid caliph once again appeared on coins and in the Friday sermons in Iran a hundred years after Hulagu's Mongols had destroyed the Baghdad caliphate.

11. Both sons, Shah Mahmud and Shah Shoja, had served their father loyally during the Azarbaijan campaign. Shah Sultan, Amir Mohammad's nephew, had captured Abu Eshaq's treasure and, later, Abu Eshaq himself at Esfahan. According to Kotbi (pp. 56–59), Amir Mohammad was infuriated because Shah Sultan had taken possession of part of the revenues of Esfahan and because his two sons, during their pursuit of enemy forces in Azarbaijan, had held a drinking party.

12. In 1367, Shah Mahmud murdered his wife when he discovered her treasonous correspondence with Shah Shoja.

13. The text of these letters is in Kotbi, p. 104 ff.

14. See above, chapter 2.

15. The bloody struggles preceding the final Mozaffarid collapse had seen the blinding of Zein al-Abedin in 1391, the death of Abu Yazid b. Amir Mohammad in 1390, the death in battle of Shah Mansur in 1393, and the slaughter of 50,000 Esfahanis by Amir Timur's forces in 1387.

16. According to one account, probably invented by later historians to teach a moral lesson, Amir Timur ordered the Mozaffarid princes to eat together on one carpet. He then asked them if they had ever eaten together that way, and one of the princes boldly answered, "If we had been so united, how could you have invaded Iraq [i.e. western Iran] in the first place?"

17. *Shadd al-Izar*, p. 114. This dome is still known as Bibi Dokhtaran in Shiraz, although the other buildings in the complex have disappeared.

18. In 1377, Shah Shoja brought Seyyed Sharif Jorjani to Shiraz to teach in this school. The famous scholar, who died in 1413, is buried in an area still called Dar al-Shafa.

19. Ibn Battuta (p. 202) says that he saw this building when he visited Shiraz in 1347 and reports that it had risen about eleven feet above the ground. According to the poet Obeid Zakani, however, who mentions the building in an ode, Abu Eshaq did not begin building it until 1353, his last year in Shiraz.

20. The books have long since disappeared. This building, in poor condition in 1972, is the subject of two monographs by A. N. Behruzi, one published in 1962 and the other in 1970, and of one by Donald Wilber of the Asia Institute.

21. In 1970, the author found this neglected site with the kind help of the inhabitants of this quarter of Shiraz. Because of the situation of the stones, however, it was not possible to take proper photographs. The identification of *Panj-tan* with the Zarkub family tomb is based on the apparent age of the stones, combined with the information about the Zarkub graves in *Shadd al-Izar*, pp. 310–319.

4. PEOPLES AND PLACES

1. In 1972, the contrast between the two parts of Shiraz was extreme. One was a city of wide streets, modern houses, expensive stores, movie theaters, restaurants, parks, hospitals, the university, and government offices. The other was a city of mosques, cemeteries, shrines, public baths, narrow alleys, *bazarchehs* (small markets), and theological schools. In this old section lay most of the remains that helped reconstruct the fourteenth-century city.

2. Angiolello and Josephat Barbaro in *Safarnameh*, pp. 84, 297. Two hundred thousand would be a reasonable population estimate of the entire Shiraz plain, including the small towns of Sarvestan, Kavar, and Khafr.

3. This estimate is based on a density of 125 persons per hectare as suggested by Russell, p. 101. *Farsnameh-ye-Naseri*, vol. II, pp. 22–3, gives the population of Shiraz (with almost the same area as the fourteenth-century town) as 53,607 in 1883. In 1956, about forty percent of the population of the Shiraz census district lived in Shiraz itself (Clarke, p. 45), but in the fourteenth century the proportion must have been lower.

4. From Ja'far Vajed, "Description of Three Verses of Sheikh Ruzbehan Baqli in Shirazi Dialect." *Rahnema-ye-Ketab*, vols. XI–XII (February–March 1970), pp. 727–30.

5. On Mowlana Shahin, see Amnon Netzer, "Literature of the Jews of Iran: A Short Survey." In *Padyavand*, vol. 1 (Los Angeles: 1996), pp. 5–17.

6. Ultimately, there were very few "native" Shirazis, and almost everyone traced ancestry to somewhere else. Shiraz was peopled by immigrants who considered themselves Shirazi within a few generations. If there were any "Mayflower" descendents in Shiraz, they were people who claimed Arab descent.

7. There were, however, mass movements of tribes. For example, during the late seventh/thirteenth century the Owghan and Jorma Mongols migrated to the Kerman region.

8. *Shadd al-Izar,* passim. The Zarkub family was originally Esfahani. The chief judge of Atabek Abu Bakr b. Sa'd was Jamal al-Din Mesri (d. 1255).

9. *Farsnameh-ye-Naseri,* vol. II, p. 20. *Nozhat al-Qolub,* p. 113. If the circumference figure is accurate, the Buyid city was much larger than the fourteenth-century Inju and Mozaffarid town, which was about 7,500 meters in circumference.

10. Agha Mohammad Khan Qajar levelled the walls of Shiraz in 1790. After some half-hearted attempts at restoration by his successors, the walls were finally destroyed in an earthquake in 1821.

11. *Nozhat al-Qolub,* p. 113.

12. Page 37. Two or three of these areas were outside the city wall.

13. The information presented is based on the following sources: (a) references to districts in literary sources from the fourteenth century or earlier; (b) extant graves and buildings from this period or earlier which can be located and identified; and (c) later descriptions of the quarters of Shiraz, which included their location, size, and population. The *Farsnameh-ye-Naseri* describes Karim Khan Zand's reorganization of the city quarters in the eighteenth century and includes pre-Zand names for some of the districts.

14. *Safarnameh,* p. 194. Shiraz has no perennial rivers, so surface water in the city would have originated from *qanats* whose tunnels ended outside the town. The water then flowed above ground through the city.

15. *Farsnameh-ye-Naseri,* vol. II, p. 21. Although this was the longest of Shiraz's *qanats,* it was so well built that it never needed repairs. Its water was always cool in summer and warm enough in the winter and late fall to raise steam from its channel.

16. For example, the Atabeks Songhor b. Mowdud (twelfth century) and Abu Bakr b. Sa'd (thirteenth century) endowed public fountains in the Songhoriyeh and Masjed Atiq areas, respectively (*Shiraznameh,* pp. 72, 85). The earliest water supply inside Shiraz of which we have definite knowledge was the old *kheirat* or *limek qanat.* Its source was over four miles north of Shiraz (*Farsnameh-ye-Naseri,* vol. II, p. 21).

17. Mostowfi writes (*Nozhat al-Qolub,* p. 113), "The city is very pleasant to live in; but its streets, by reason that nowadays the people have no privies, are very filthy, hence it is impossible to anyone to go about in these streets and not be defiled."

18. In the fourteenth century this mosque was flourishing, second in importance only to the Old Congregational Mosque. Among the outstanding preachers there were Sheikh Zia al-Din Baghnovi (d. 743/1342) and Qazi Jamal al-Din Mesri (d. 1255), chief judge of Fars under Atabek Abu Bakr b. Sa'd. This mosque was the center of a complex of buildings built by Atabek Songhor b. Mowdud in the twelfth century in the Khargah-Tarashan (tentmakers') quarter in the Bagh-e-Now district.

19. As befits such an important mosque, the Jame' Atiq always had a number of preachers. In the twelfth century, the positions of imam and khatib had long been in the family of Naser al-Din Sharabi (*Shiraznameh,* p. 67). In the thirteenth and fourteenth centuries many members of Joneid Shirazi's family (the Baghnovis) preached there, although one of the most famous of his ancestors, Sheikh Sadr al-Din Mozaffar

(d. 1289), refused invitations to preach at the Jame' Atiq, preferring to stay at his own small, family mosque in the Bagh-e-Now district. Joneid's cousin, Rokn al-Din Yahya (d. 1368), was appointed *khatib* of the Jame' Atiq by Shah Abu Esheq. Other outstanding preachers in this mosque included Amir Asil al-Din Alavi (d. 1286) and his great-grandson, Amir Seif al-Din Yusef Va'ez (d. 1362).

20. *Shadd al-Izar,* pp. 442, 304, 332, 196.

21. *Farsnameh-ye-Naseri,* vol. II, p. 162. The founder named the school after his son, Ghiyath al-Din Mansour. By the nineteenth century this school had lost most of its endowment to various usurpers. Nader Shah, for example, in the eighteenth century converted much of the endowment into royal holdings. In 1972 the building and grounds were in very poor condition.

22. See above, chapter 1. Khwajeh Amid al-Din was executed in 1227. The Dar al-Shafa School took its name from its site, originally occupied by the tenth-century Azodiyeh Hospital.

23. For example, a disciple of Sheikh Najm al-Din Mahmud Sarduz (d. 1298) endowed a *rabat* for his master in the Bagh-e-Ootlogh quarter, where the sheikh himself, his father (d. 1253), and his son (d. fourteenth century) are all buried. *Shiraz-nameh,* p. 184; *Shadd al-Izar,* pp. 261–63.

24. *Safarnameh,* p. 205, notes the existence of a school and pilgrims' lodge next to Sheikh-e-Kabir's tomb.

25. *Safarnameh,* p. 194. No trace of this main bazaar is left, but it occupied the approximate site of the 1972 Bazar-e-Haji, which ends in an area between the Jame' Atiq and the tomb of Mohammad b. Musa.

26. *Mokatebat-e-Rashidi,* pp. 252–6. Najm al-Din and his descendants were all well-known physicians who composed works on medicine, including the fourteenth-century Persian *Kafayeh-ye-Mojahediyeh,* written by Mansur b. Mohammad, the grandson of Najm al-Din's nephew, for the ruler Zein al-Abedin b. Shah Shoja Mozaffari. *Shadd al-Izar,* pp. 277–80.

27. In the fourteenth century the wealth of Shiraz also supported the prosperity and culture of the Il-Khanid courts at Tabriz and Soltaniyeh. When Rashid al-Din established his Rob'-e-Rashidi (Rashidi Quarter) in Tabriz at the beginning of the fourteenth century, he brought two hundred Qoran-readers there and settled them in two districts to the left and the right of the *gonbad* (tower). Those on the right were supported by the income of *waqf* (endowment) property in Shiraz. *Mokatebat-e-Rashidi,* p. 318.

28. *Divan,* p. 170 ff. Moslem Shirazis have forgotten most of these specialties, but in 1972 the Jews of Shiraz still prepared *khaleh-bibi* (p. 179) and *gondi* (p. 176). The Jews of Kurdestan still made *sokhtu* (p. 178); the Moslems of Borujerd made the same dish, calling it *soghdun.*

29. Not all Shirazi dishes were so appetizing. The poet gives a recipe for *mahiyeh* that calls for "fish water and various garbage that the body-washers of Lar know." The bread eaten with this food was called "the wasted"; attempts to make this dish were called "the futile"; and the house where it was made was called the "abode of misery."

30. *Nozhat al-Qolub,* pp. 117, 126.

31. These figures come from *Farsnameh-ye-Ibn Balkhi* and *Nozhat al-Qolub*. All figures are expressed in "currency dinars" *(dinar-e-rayej)* of the Il-Khanid period, which were equivalent to about 3/7 of the Abbasid dinar. See *Nozhat al-Qolub*, pp. 33–4.

32. Ayati-Vassaf, 263. A *kharvar* of Shiraz equaled about 3.32 kilograms. Petrushevsky, vol. I, p. 140.

33. *Nozhat al-Qolub*, p. 33.

34. *Nozhat al-Qolub*, p. 33. Twenty-five years later, Shah Mahmud Mozaffari, writing to his brother Shah Shoja, complained that in their division of the kingdom he had been given only the *kharabeh* (ruins) of Esfahan, devastated by constant invasions, while Shah Shoja had taken the richer province of Fars. (Kotbi, pp. 82–3).

35. This increase, although difficult to document, must have been related to the political and social instability of Fars that began in the eleventh century, and which brought a decline in both productivity and population. Insecurity increased the government's need for revenue, while the same insecurity decreased the tax base in the population.

36. Cited in Lambton, *Landlord and Peasant in Persia*, pp. 82–4. In 1318 revenue agents' exactions in Firuzabad resulted in the abandonment of 33 prosperous villages which had paid more than 30,000 dinars of taxes. Ayati-Vassaf, pp. 361–2.

37. *Tarikh-e-Mobarak-e-Ghazani*, p. 269.

38. Vol. II, pp. 261–305. The exact nature of many of these taxes is unclear.

39. I am indebted to Mr. Ja'far Vajad of Shiraz for helping me decipher the beautiful *sols* script of this inscription, and to Mr. Mas'ud Farzad of Pahlavi University for explaining some of the terms used. It is obvious from the text that it was more profitable for governments to tax sin than to forbid it. Lest any tax be overlooked, the inscription concludes, "and any other traditional or new taxes from the time of the late ruler Shahrokh Mirza [r. 1409–1447] and Padeshah Ebrahim [his governor of Fars]."

5. THE CITY ADMINISTRATION

1. For Shirazis, security did not always mean resisting outside attacks. The city sometimes changed rulers without a fight in a deal between rival pretenders or by agreement of influential officials.

2. For the text and translation of this poem, see Browne, *A Literary History of Persia*, vol. III, pp. 275–76.

3. See above, chapter 3.

4. See above, chapter 3.

5. *Shiraznameh*, p. 187. Baliyan is a village six miles south of Kazeroun. For an account of this family, see Qazvini's notes to *Shadd al-Izar*, pp. 484–7.

6. On this question of Turk and Iranian, see the excellent discussion entitled "A Bicultural Society" in Larry Potter's unpublished thesis, *The Kart Dynasty of Heart: Religion and Politics in Medieval Iran*, Columbia University, 1992, pp. 141–48.

7. Tashi Khatun, the mother of Shah Sheikh Abu Eshaq, and Makhdum Shah Khan Qotlogh, the mother of Shah Shoja, were both Turkish. In 1346, when Abu Eshaq paid a visit to the elderly chief judge of Fars, Qazi Majd al-Din Esma'il Fali,

the ruler sat opposite the judge holding his ears. This action was a sign of great honor, since the Mongol commanders acted thus only in the presence of their sultan (Ibn Battuta, pp. 195, 198).

8. Ibn Battuta, pp. 194, 199–200.

9. *Farsnameh-ye-Naseri,* vol. I, p. 59.

10. See, for example, Enjavi Shirazi, pp. 51–3, and Zarin-Kub, p. 51.

11. See above, chapter 2.

12. Ideally, the minister served as an intermediary between the Turkish ruler and his Iranian subjects. See above, chapter 1, concerning ministers of Iranian origin serving the Turkish Salghurids. On the ideal conduct of a minister see *Qabusnameh,* pp. 159–63.

13. Setudeh, vol. I, pp. 80, 84–5. The poet Khaju Kermani dedicated a number of his compositions to Shams al-Din and his son. Setudeh, vol. I, p. 80.

14. *Tarikh-e-Yazd,* pp. 118–19, 239. This minister endowed a school in Yazd which Amir Mohammad Mozaffar destroyed out of enmity for Abu Eshaq.

15. Hafez is using *abjad* numerology, which assigns value to the letters of امیذ جود. The resulting value is 764 A. H., or 1363 C.E.

16. See above, chapter 3. Considering Amir Mohammad's character, remaining in his favor for such a long time was no small accomplishment. In addition to being bloodthirsty, fanatical, suspicious, and evil-tempered, he "used curses that made muledrivers blush" (Ghani, p. 187).

17. See above, chapter 3.

18. Zarin-Kub, p. 38. The most important court poets were Khaju Kermani and Obeid Zakani, both older than Hafez.

19. Setudeh, vol. I, p. 160; Ghani, pp. 268–9. Twenty-four leaves of this Qoran have survived and in 1972 were in the Pars Museum in Shiraz.

20. In Islamic tradition, Asef was the name of the minister of King Solomon. The sources refer to Fars in the thirteenth and fourteenth centuries as the Molk-e-Soleiman (Kingdom of Solomon). See Melikian, "Le Royaume de Salomon."

21. See Bulliet, *The Patricians of Nishapur,* p. 61.

22. Abu Eshaq's execution of city notables during the siege of 1352–53 (see above, chapter 3), is a clear case of this local exercise of royal power. On a higher level, in the thirteenth century Atabek Abu Bakr dismissed the chief judge of Fars, from the Alavi family, and replaced him with a member of the (related) Fali-Sirafi family (Ayati-Vassaf, p. 96; see above, chapter 5).

23. In Nishapur in the tenth and eleventh centuries the *ra'is* was a very important figure of the civil administration who acted something like a mayor. The *ra'is* of Nishapur was usually a member of one of the most powerful local families. Bulliet, *The Patricians of Nishapur,* pp. 66–7.

24. *Farsnameh-ye-Ibn Balkhi* (Damghani), pp. 152–3. I could find no other record of this family, whose name points to an Iranian origin.

25. Ibid., p. 153.

26. There were more fundamental reasons than the union of the Mardasa and Afzari families for the fusion of the two offices and the *qazi*'s power eclipsing that of the *ra'is.* Since Shiraz had been the capital of minor dynasties almost continuously

since Buyid times, there was little need for a purely civil official such as the *ra'is* to act as an intermediary between the city and a distant capital.

27. Ayati-Vassaf, p. 96. Also see above, chapter 2.

28. Ibn Battuta, vol. II, pp. 302–4.

29. Lambton, pp. 98–9.

30. Ibn Battuta, vol. II, pp. 304–5.

31. *Mokatebat-e-Rashidi,* p. 56 ff.

32. *Ta'rifat, Divan,* vol. II, p. 158. In his *Resaleh-ye-Delgosha,* Obeid tells humorous anecdotes about several well-known judges of Shiraz. These stories, if not exactly obscene, show a lighter side of their personalities.

33. See above, chapter 3. Hafez Abru, cited by Qazvini in notes to *Shadd al-Izar,* p. 362.

34. Ibn Battuta, pp. 195–198.

35. See map in *Farsnameh-ye-Naseri,* vol. II, pp. 17–18. Fal is the name of a region near the coast of the Persian Gulf behind the port of Siraf, an area now called Kalehdar or Galehdar (ibid., vol. II, p. 227). Afzar (or Afzār) is another region of the *garmsir* lying southeast of Shiraz between Qir and Khonj on the road to the Persian Gulf (ibid., vol. II, p. 179). Beiza is a region of the *sardsir* located northwest of Shiraz (ibid., vol. II, pp. 182–3). It is possible that there were in fact two, rather than three, families of judges, since the family of Fali-Sirafi may have been descendents of the Fazari family. The minister of Atabek Sa'd b. Zangi, Amid al-Din As'ad Afzari (see above, chapter 1), must have been part of the family of the Fazari judges. The minister's descendent, Safi al-Din Abu al-Kheir Mas'ud b. Mahmud b. Abu Fath Fali Sirafi (d. 1279), was related to the first Qazi Majd al-Din Esma'il. The son of Safi al-Din, Mowlana Qotb al-Din Fali (d. 1312), composed the famous *Sharh-e-Qasideh-ye-Amidiyeh* on a work of his ancestor. (See above, chapter 1, note 20.) For more information about this branch of the powerful Fali-Sirafi family see *Shadd al-Izar,* pp. 430–5, and *Shiraznameh,* p. 202.

36. The clearest sign of the power of the Fali-Sirafis is the fact that only rarely was someone not a prince, minister, or chief judge able to afford endowing a major seminary. See above, chapter 4.

37. Ayati-Vassaf, 96.

38. Ayati-Vassaf, p. 120. As far as the sources go, this compromise was a unique instance of a jointly held chief-judgeship. In fact, as Vassaf adds, Rokn al-Din took precedence in spite of the arrangement.

39. Historians may have overemphasized these incidents and exaggerated the power of the *qazi* out of wishful thinking for an ideal Islamic state, where everyone, including the ruler, would be subject to the *qazi*'s rulings on Islamic law.

40. In 1356, Shah Sheikh Abu Eshaq, though weakened, was still a threat to the Mozaffarids.

41. Ibn Battuta, pp. 204–5. The close association of the Alavis and Shiraz was a result of the presence of the tombs of three brothers of Imam Reza in the city. Many of the great *seyyed*s of Shiraz were buried in the *Jame' Atiq* area, near the graves of Amir Ahmad b. Musa and his brother Mohammad.

42. *Shiraznameh,* p. 153.

43. *Shadd al-Izar*, pp. 292–3; *Shiraznameh*, p. 202.

44. *Shadd al-Izar*, p. 171. The sources do not say whether Seyyed Taj al-Din inherited his father's position of *naqib*.

45. *Shadd al-Izar*, p. 325; *Shiraznameh*, p. 202.

46. Ayati-Vassaf, p. 96.

47. *Shiraznameh*, pp. 201–2. Zeid Asud had married a daughter of Azod al-Dowleh Al-e-Buyeh. His descendant Abi Mo'ali's dates are uncertain, but he probably lived in the early twelfth century.

48. Our information about the family relationships of the *seyyed*s of Shiraz is incomplete. We know that they married both Alavis and non-Alavis—see, for example, the genealogy of the family of Amir Asil al-Din Alavi-Mohammadi in the appendix. But the exact relationship between family and the office of *naqib* is unclear.

49. For the fourteenth-century usage of the word *kalu* (variant *kolu*), which has disappeared from modern Persian, see *Loghatnameh-ye-Dehkhoda*, vol. XI, p. 16, 313.

50. Ibn Battuta, p. 199.

51. Hafez Abru, p. 168; Kotbi, p. 39.

52. From *Jame' al-Tavarikh*, cited by Ghani, pp. 123–4.

53. *Farsnameh-ye-Naseri*, vol. I, p. 59.

54. Zarrin-Kub, p. 1, calls Shiraz in this period *shahr-e-rendan*, or city of the *rend*s. The leaders of the street mobs were the popular heroes called *pahlevanan* (strong men, wrestlers), who were often associated with the *zurkhaneth* (athletic societies). In the fourteenth century, military officers also held the title *pahlavan*. For example, Shah Shoja's governor of Kerman was called Pahlevan Asad (Kotbi, p. 86). In recent times, mob leaders have been called *chaqu-keshan* (knife-pullers) by their opponents and *pahlavanan* by their supporters.

55. *Javanmardi* resembles the Arabic *futuwwa*, and the *pahlavan*s of Shiraz resembled the *akhi*s of Anatolia, described in Ibn Battuta, vol. II, pp. 418–21.

56. See above, chapter 2.

57. According to Joneid Shirazi, in *Shadd al-Izar*, p. 198, all local rulers were terrified of his tongue.

58. Ibid., p. 201.

59. Bulliet, "Shaikh," suggests that the Sheikh al-Eslam was the head of the educational system with the power to certify teacher's credentials. But the sources do not mention the Sheikh al-Eslam's performing such a function in Shiraz. The biographies of the Sheikh al-Eslams of Shiraz emphasize their positions as preachers and as sufi leaders, while calling the most famous teachers Mowlana.

60. *Shadd al-Izar*, p. 124; *Shiraznameh*, pp. 159–9. These sources say that Qotb al-Din was "popularly called Sheikh al-Eslam." He also held the sufi title *Sheikh al-Shoyukh*.

61. *Shadd al-Izar*, p. 353; *Shiraznameh*, p. 181. He preached for sixty years in the Songhoriyeh Mosque, and was Sheikh al-Eslam at the time of the writing of the *Shiraznameh* in 745/1344.

62. In the case of the political leaders, the author writes of their piety and support of religion, not their military deeds.

63. *Shiraznameh*, pp. 168–9.

64. Names such as Ruzbeh, Salbeh, and Nikruz were common Iranian names in

Fars. The sheikhs of Beiza, for example, traced their ancestry to a certain Salbeh, and Qazi Majd al-Din Esma'il Fali (d. 1268) was known as Ibn Nikruz, after some distant ancestor. The Baghnovis, who called themselves Qoreishi after the Arab tribe of the Prophet, had intermarried with the natives of Fars, and the first of the family to come to Shiraz from Fasa in the twelfth century was named Sheikh Zein al-Din Mozaffar b. Ruzbehan.

65. The sources mention only one case of intermarriage between these groups— between Sheikh Najib al-Din b. Bozghash (1197–1279) and a daughter of Seyyed Qazi Sharaf al-Din Mohammad, chief judge and son of the *naqib* of Fars (*Shadd al-Izar,* p. 335).

66. This distinction between "upper" and "lower" local aristocrats is based chiefly on their differing treatment in the sources and on details such as burial site (for example, the Jame' Atiq area was more prestigious for burial than Dar al-Salam) and association with mosques and schools. Preaching in the Songhoriyeh Mosque or the Old Congregational Mosque carried more prestige than, for example, preaching in the more modest mosque of Haj Ali Assar.

67. One Imam of a small mosque in the Kazeroun Gate area said such long prayers that he had only a very small congregation (*Shadd al-Izar,* p. 118).

6. SHIRAZI SOCIETY

1. Moqaddasi, cited by Bosworth, *Ghaznavids,* p. 166.

2. Bulliet, *The Patricians of Nishapur,* pp. 78–81.

3. *Nozhat al-Qolub* (Persian text), pp. 53–4.

4. *Nozhat al-Qolub* (Persian text), p. 54. Dardasht and Jubareh are quarters of Esfahan.

5. Ibid., p. 148. In other words, in the fourteenth century do-hava'i was an Esfahani custom, and not characteristic of Fars.

6. Kotbi, p. 91. The former supported Mahmud's brother Shah Shoja, while the latter supported his nephew Sultan Oveis b. Shah Shoja. The names *chahar-dangeh* and *do-dangeh* may refer to specific Esfahani factions or to the proportions of the population supporting each contender.

7. Kotbi, p. 86. Pahlavan Asad and Makhdum Shah's dispute began when the former supported a Khorasani wrestler and the latter supported a Kermani wrestler.

8. *Farsnameh-ye-Naseri,* vol. II, p. 22, and Perry, pp. 53–55. The latter provides a map showing the Heidari and Neimati quarters in the eighteenth century. It is possible that the Safavids created these factions to facilitate their own rule by dividing and thus weakening a hostile Sunni population. Today, Iranian children call their equivalent of "cops and robbers" *heidari-neimati.*

9. See above, chapter 5. Also *Shadd al-Izar,* pp. 176–79.

10. He was related to Khwajeh Ahmad Khasseh (d. fourteenth century), part of the family of the founders of the Khasseh Mosque in the Bahaliyeh district (*Shadd al-Izar,* p. 107).

11. See above, chapter 2. The best account of this incident is in Hafez Abru, p.

168. *Shiraznameh,* pp. 114–15, adds details, although the author was clearly biased in favor of the Injus.

12. See above, chapter 3.

13. If Shiraz had been thus divided, what would have been the basis for its division? The city could not have been split over law schools *(mazhab);* by the fourteenth century, most Shirazis were Sunnis of the Shafe'i school, with only a few being Hanafis or Shi'ites (*Nozhat al-Qolub,* p. 113). Furthermore, by the time of Hafez the distinction and the rivalry between the law schools was not as sharp as it had been earlier. Some such rivalry had existed in Shiraz during the twelfth century, when the trusteeship of the endowment of the school of Zahedeh Khatun was first given to the leader (imam) of the Hanafis, but was later turned over to the Shafe'i leader (*Shiraznameh,* p. 67). The great chief judges of Shiraz in the thirteenth and fourteenth century were Shafe'i, but gave judgements in more than one school. Qazi Majd al-Din Esma'il Fali-Sirafi, for example, who was chief judge under Atabeg Abu Bakr in the thirteenth century, "followed both the schools of Shafe'i and Abu Hanifeh in his judgements" (Ayati-Vassaf, p. 96). Qazi Borhan al-Din Osman Kuhgiluye'i (d. 1380), chief judge under Shah Shoja, was himself a Shafe'i, but "gave opinions in the four schools" (Kotbi, p. 81, *Shadd al-Izar,* p. 361).

14. The factions of nineteenth-century Shiraz probably do not originate earlier than the Safavid period, when the imposed conversion to Shi'ism may have led the rulers to encourage the formation of factions among their subjects, using the already existing institution of the neighborhood.

15. See above, chapter 2, for an example of this competition during the period of direct Mongol rule in the late thirteenth century. The process of division into factions loyal to powerful rival individuals or families has always been at work in Iran. In the twentieth century Shiraz witnessed struggles between the Qavamis and the Qashga'is, and, at a lower level, between competing groups at Shiraz (then Pahlavi) University. For a fictionalized account of the conflicts in the early twentieth century, see Simin Daneshvar's novel *Su va Shun.* On the conflicts at Shiraz University see Bill, pp. 78–87.

16. *Nozhat al-Qolub,* p. 113, *Hezar Mazar,* pp. 3–4; *Shadd al-Izar,* p. 3.

17. Ibn Battuta, pp. 204–5.

18. Ibid., p. 205. The tomb of Tashi Khatun's husband, Mahmud Shah Inju (d. 1335), adjoined this shrine.

19. In 1972 the inhabitants no longer cared about learning Arabic grammar, but believed that yoghurt eaten from a depression in the grave stone would cure whooping cough in children.

20. Ibn Battuta, pp. 207–8. According to the author, "Nowhere on earth is the Qoran read so beautifully as in Shiraz."

21. *Shadd al-Izar,* pp. 409–11.

22. Ibid., pp. 259–60.

23. Ibid., pp. 346–7. See above, chapter 2.

24. *Shadd al-Izar,* p. 176; *Shiraznameh,* p. 176. Faqih Sa'en al-Din was the author of the lost *Tarikh-e-Mashayekh-e-Fars,* a major source for Joneid's *Shadd al-Izar.*

25. *Hezar-Mazar,* p. 63.

26. *Shadd al-Izar,* p. 109. After a visit to Sheikh Amin al-Din Baliyani in Kazeroun (see above, chapter 5), he returned to Shiraz and became both a poet and a very eloquent preacher. According to Zarin-kub, p. 19, this incident is the origin of the legend that the poet Hafez (whose name was also Shams al-Din Mohammad) was illiterate.

27. *Shadd al-Izar,* pp. 92–93.

28. For the wide variety of meanings of *rend,* see Sajadi, pp. 234–35. Here we use it to mean those persons who ignored the demands and constraints of religion and society. For a later version of the *rendan,* see the chapter "Among the Kalandars" in E. G. Browne's *A Year Amongst the Persians.*

29. See above, chapter 4. For the meaning and derivation of *kharabat,* see Raja'i, p. 101 ff.

30. See Sajadi, pp. 281–86.

31. In modern Persian, weak tea has "seen a policeman" *(azhandideh)* and has lost its color out of fright. Hafez's *mohtaseb* is probably none other than Mobarez al-Din Mozaffar.

32. *Nozhat al-Qolub,* p. 113.

33. *Shadd al-Izar,* p. 89. This was Sheikh Jalal al-Din Mas'ud (d. 1325), a brother of the famous preacher Rokn al-Din Mansur Rastgu (see above, chapter 5).

34. *Shadd al-Izar,* p. 416.

35. *Shadd al-Izar,* p. 377. Late in life, Sheikh Rostam settled in Ja'farabad, north of the city, where Amir Pir Hosein Chupani built a home for him.

36. *Shadd al-Izar,* p. 173. This ascetic *seyyed*'s brother was Taj al-Din Ja'far (d. ca. 1354), one of the most powerful men in Shiraz (see above, chapter 5).

37. The value placed on diversity in Shiraz is best illustrated by a story about Torkan Khatun, the daughter of Atabek Sa'd b. Zangi. She once visited Sheikh Mo'ayyed al-Din (a noted ascetic) and found him wearing rough, heavy clothes in the summer. But when she visited Sheikh Sadr al-Din Mozaffar Baghnovi, she saw him wearing fine, thin garments. When she questioned Sheikh Mo'ayyed, asking how two holy men could be so different, the sheikh answered, "Both of us are men of God, for the ways of God are as many as the number of men" (*Shadd al-Izar,* p. 254).

38. On this question, see chapter 10, "Moderate Shi'ism" (pp. 258–91), in Petrushevsky's *Islam in Iran* (Persian translation).

39. *Nozhat al-Qolub,* passim.

40. *Shadd al-Izar,* pp. 301, 325. On the family relationship of these two figures, see the genealogies in the appendix. The Alavi family members, despite their descent from the house of Ali, were, as patricians of Shiraz, adamant upholders of Sunnism.

41. The aristocracy of Shiraz (or at least those members recorded in the sources) was strongly Sunni. Neither of the two major biographical works of this period, *Shadd al-Izar* and *Shiraznameh,* give any notice to Shia scholars or judges.

42. Ayati-Vassaf, pp. 110–11. On this occasion Shiraz barely escaped a general massacre.

43. *Shadd al-Izar,* p. 271. Petrushevsky (p. 373) claims that these Shi'ite messianic

expectations were based on a social revolutionary movement to overthrow oppressive Sunni governments.

44. For the founding of these shrines, see above, chapter 1. In the fourteenth century, Tashi Khatun, Abu Eshaq's mother, was a particular devotee of Ahmad b. Musa.

45. *Shiraznameh,* pp. 190–95.

46. The *Sahih* of al-Bokhari is one of the authoritative Sunni collections of *hadith.* The *Masabih al-Sonnat* was a collection of tradition by Hosein b. Mas'ud (d. ca. 1121), called Mohiy al-Sonnat ("the reviver of tradition"). The father of Sheikh Rokn al-Din, Sheikh Sadr al-Din Mozaffar Baghnovi (d. 1289), composed a commentary on the *Masabih* (*Shadd al-Izar,* p. 192).

47. This book was written by Sheikh Shahab al-Din Omar b. Mohammad Sohravardi (d. 1235), one of the family of the famous sufi masters of Baghdad. Sheikh Zahir al-Din's father, the learned Najib al-Din Ali b. Bozghash (594–678/1198–1279), studied *Awaref al-Ma'aref* under Sheikh Sohravardi himself and received his *ejazeh* directly from the author (*Shiraznameh,* p. 177).

48. *Shadd al-Izar,* pp. 400–1.

49. This book was written by Najm al-Din Abd al-Ghaffar Qazvini (d. 1267). See Qazvini, notes to *Shadd al-Izar,* p. 71.

50. See above, chapter 1, note 20.

51. *Shadd al-Izar,* p. 77. Concerning Qazi Beiza'i, see above, chapter 5.

52. On the role of the sufi master, see above, chapter 6.

53. *Shadd al-Izar,* pp. 385–6.

54. Concerning Shah Shoja's attendance, see Kotbi, p. 81. About Hafez's attendance, see Gol-Andam's preface to his collection of Hafez's poems, cited by Browne, *Literary History,* vol. III, p. 272.

55. *Shadd al-Izar,* pp. 106, 270, 414.

56. *Shadd al-Izar,* pp. 71–2. Jamal al-Din Kuhgiluye'i was the author of a summary of the *Havi al-Saghir.*

57. From *Selseleh al-Nasab-e-Safaviyyeh,* cited by Browne, vol. III, pp. 484–5.

58. *Shadd al-Izar,* pp. 385, 304.

59. Mowlana Qavam al-Din's father, Mowlana Najm al-Din Faqih, was also a noted teacher, who had taught *adab* to one of his son's contemporaries, Mohammad b. Hasan Jowhari (*Shadd al-Izar,* pp. 378–9). Emam Naser al-Din's father, Zia al-Din Mas'ud Shirazi, had been an important sufi leader (*Shadd al-Izar,* pp. 68–70). Najib al-Din's father was a wealthy Turkish merchant who had settled in Shiraz during the Salghurid period (*Shadd al-Izar,* p. 334).

60. *Shadd al-Izar,* pp. 58–9.

61. *Shadd al-Izar,* p. 385.

62. *Shadd al-Izar,* pp. 355–56. The custom of wearing unusual clothes to call attention to injustice was not new in Iran in the Salghurid period. The *Siyasatnameh* (pp. 13–16) relates how a ruler ordered all those persons who had been oppressed to wear red clothes so that he could distinguish them easily.

63. For further reading in the subject, see R. Nicholson's *Islamic Mysticism,* H. Nasr's *Three Islamic Sages,* and innumerable books in Persian, including Ghani's *Tarikh-e-Tasavvof dar Eslam.*

64. See, for example, the beautiful, mysterious lyric which begins:

سالها دل طلب جام جم از ما میکرد وانچه خود داشت از بیگانه تمنا میکرد

For years, my heart sought the magic cup of Jamshid,
Seeking what it already possessed from others.

65. *Divan,* p. 174. The passage parodies most of the common sufi practices and expressions. For their meaning in sufism, see Raja'i, *Farhang-e-Ash'ar-e-Hafez.*

66. In Hafez's time, Ibn Khafif's tomb was an important center of pilgrimage and scholarship. Concerning the life and works of Ibn Khafif, see Arberry, *Shiraz,* pp. 61–85; *Shadd al-Izar,* pp. 38–46; *Shiraznameh,* pp. 125–30.

67. Arberry, *Shiraz,* p. 74.

68. *Shadd al-Izar,* pp. 58, 124–5; *Shiraznameh,* pp. 158–9. Concerning Kathki's three famous pupils, see above, chapter 6.

69. The Shafe'i school was the favorite of most sufis. See Arberry, *Shiraz,* p. 103, and Bulliet, *The Patricians of Nishapur,* pp. 42–3.

70. For a detailed discussion of the sufi *kherqeh* and the customs associated with it, see Raja'i, pp. 122–57.

71. For a list of these references, see Raja'i, pp. 156–7.

72. *Shiraznameh,* p. 127.

73. *Shiraznameh,* p. 154; *Shadd al-Izar,* p. 300. Sheikh Saraj al-Din traced his own sufi *selseleh* to the great Sheikh Morshed, Abu Eshaq Kazeruni (d. 1035). As with *ejazehs,* a disciple could receive *kherqehs* from more than one sufi master.

74. *Shadd al-Izar,* pp. 317–18, 198. The grave of Sheikh Yusef is still extant in Sarvestan (*Farsnameh-ye-Naseri,* vol. II, p. 221).

75. *Shadd al-Izar,* p. 339.

76. At best, these sufis would use their wealth and influence for charity. At worst, they would line their pockets and adorn their *khaneqahs.* See Enjavi-Shirazi, pp. 60–61.

77. *Shadd al-Izar,* p. 109. This Sheikh Shams al-Din later became wealthy and, after returning from Kazeroun, founded a *khaneghah* in Shiraz. He became a member of the lower aristocracy, and his son, Fakhr al-Din Ahmad (d. ca. 1364), also became a famous sheikh (*Shadd al-Izar,* p. 110).

78. The direct relationship between culture (especially poetry) and political instability has been noted by Browne, *Literary History,* vol. III, pp. 160–1, 207.

79. Gray, *Persian Painting,* pp. 57–59. According to Gray, "These miniatures reflect a style which was current in Iran before the Mongol invasions, exemplified in the lustre-painted pottery, tiles, and vessels, examples of which go back to the second half of the twelfth century." Among the specifically Iranian features of the Shiraz school of painting were heavy outline of features; filling in of backgrounds with foliage; firm, lively animal drawing; symmetry, hierarchy, and frontality; and the rouged cheeks and strongly marked beards and eyebrows of the men. Among the new features in the painting were the use of peony blossoms and of conical, colored mountains.

80. See above, chapters 3 and 4.

81. *Hezar Mazar,* p. 20. See above, chapter 4.

82. *Farsnameh-ye-Naseri,* vol. II, pp. 134–5.

83. *Shadd al-Izar,* pp. 424, 364.

84. For a description of Qazi Azod al-Din's life and work, see Setudeh, vol. II, pp. 285–87. Obeid Zakani frequently mentions him in a humorous context in *Resaleh-ye-Delgosha.* Hafez praises him (in *Rejal-e-Mamlekat-e-Fars*) as follows:

دگر شهنشه دانش عضد که در تصنیف   بنای کار موافق بنام شاه نهاد

And Azod al-Din, the king of knowledge,
Who in composition dedicated the *Mawaqef* to the king.

85. Iranian critics continue to write and argue about the real meaning and significance of Hafez's work. Two interesting contemporary studies (especially for the social historian) are Zarin-Kub's *Az Kucheh-ye-Rendan* (1970) and Eslami-Nodushan's *Majara-ye-Payan-na-pazir Hafez* (1989).

86. Browne, *Literary History,* vol. III, pp. 207–353, discusses the literary merits of the poets of this period. Setudeh, vol. II, pp. 294 ff, discusses their relations with the historical figures of the era.

87. Introduction to vol. II of Obeid's *Divan* p. 4.

88. Mas'ud Farzad *(Rats against Cats)* and A. J. Arberry *(Classical Persian Literature,* pp. 291–6) have translated the entire poem. The meaning of the fable is still a mystery, although Abbas Eqbal suggests it is a parody of Amir Mobarez al-Din Mohammad, who was famous for both his bloodthirstiness and the strictness of his religious observances (Introduction to vol. I of Obeid's *Divan,* p. xvii).

89. See above, chapter 3, for his poem in praise of Abu Eshaq's emulation of the famous Taq-e-Kisra of Ctesiphon.

7. A VERY SPECIAL PLACE

1. See above, chapter 1.

2. Bausani, *The Persians,* p. 139, proposes the second hypothesis.

APPENDIX

1. Sources for the genealogies of the Shirazi family appear in table 5.3.

2. Uncertain relationships are indicated by dotted lines in the genealogies.

3. *Shadd al-Izar,* pp. 227–30.

4. See above, table 5.3., and chapter 6.

5. Another member of this family of the sheikhs of Beiza—Sheikh Saraj al-Din Mahmud b. Khalifeh (d. 562/1167)—had been the sufi master of Sheikh Ruzbehan Baqli (*Shadd al-Izar,* p. 300).

6. For biographies of Sheikh Sadr al-Din Mozaffar, see *Shadd al-Izar,* p. 190 ff, and *Shiraznameh,* p. 178 ff.

7. *Shadd al-Izar,* p. 129; *Shiraznameh,* p. 184

8. See above, chapter 6.

9. *Shadd al-Izar,* p. 210.

10. *Shadd al-Izar,* p. 208.

11. *Shadd al-Izar,* pp. 442–3; *Shiraznameh,* p. 172. See above, chapter 4.

12. Ayati-Vassaf, p. 96. According to *Shiraznameh* (p. 127), this Qazi Majd al-Din was the son of Qazi Saraj al-Din Mokarram. However, other sources (Ayati-Vassaf, *Shadd al-Izar, Mojmal-e-Fasihi*) all refer to him as Qazi Esma'il b. Nikruz. Who was Nikruz? Perhaps a more distant (Deilamite or Zoroastrian?) ancestor of this family.

13. See above, chapter 2. For a biography of Qazi Rokn al-Din, see *Shadd al-Izar,* p. 422.

14. See above, chapter 5.

15. See above, chapter 1. For a biography of Mowlana Qotb al-Din, see *Shadd al-Izar,* pp. 432–5.

16. *Shiraznameh,* p. 202. See above, tables 4.4 and 5.1.

17. The most detailed biographic notice of Amir al-Din is found in *Shadd al-Izar,* pp. 325–29. Also, see above, table 5.3.

18. According to Eqbal (notes to *Shadd al-Izar,* pp. 325–6) this Abu al-Vaqt was the most famous *hadith* scholar of his age, since he possessed the shortest chain of teachers linking him to great Bokhari (d. 869).

19. See above, chapter 1.

20. In 1972 his grave still existed in the small lane called Kucheh-ye-Lashkari near the Old Congregational Mosque.

21. *Shadd al-Izar,* pp. 300–1.

22. *Shadd al-Izar,* p. 302.

23. *Shadd al-Izar,* pp. 128–9. One of Amir Seif al-Din sons, Amir Jalal al-Din, was an acquaintance of Joneid Shirazi and was famous for his rigid and orthodox views.

BIBLIOGRAPHY

PRIMARY ARABIC AND PERSIAN SOURCES
(Dates of publication are the Iranian solar year unless otherwise noted.)

آیتی ،عبد المحمد، مصحح. تحریر تاریخ وصاف . تهران، بنیاد فرهنگ ایران،

شمارهٔ ۱۸. ۱۳۴۹.

Ayati, Abd al-Mohammad, editor. *Tahrir-e-Tarikh-e-Vassaf.* Ayati has clarified and rewrit-
ten Vassaf's bombastic and obscure original, and has created a valuable source on the
complicated social and political history of Fars in the second half of the thirteenth
century.

ابن بطوطه. سفرنامه. بترجمهٔ م. ع. موحد. تهران، بنگاهٔ ترجمه و نشر

کتاب. ۱۳۳۷

Ibn Battuta, *Safarnameh,* translated by A. Movahhed. The author visited Shiraz in 1327
and 1347, and reported valuable information on Shiraz under the Mongols and the
Injus. The account of his meeting with Qazi Majd al-Din Esma'il Fali is especially
important.

ابن البلخی. فارسنامه. بتصحیح علی نقی بهروزی. شیران، سندیکای

انتشارات، ۱۳۴۲.

Ibn al-Balkhi, *Farsnameh.* Edited by Ali Naqi Behruzi. An important source for the
history of Fars in the early Islamic period, written around 1100.

ابن حوقل. صورت العرض. بترجمهٔ جعفر شعار. تهران، بنیاد فرهنگ ایران،

۱۳۴۵.

Ibn Howqal, *Surat al-Arz.* Translated by Ja'far Sho'ar. A geographical work composed
in the tenth century.

استخری، ابو اسحق ابراهیم. *مسالک و ممالک*. بتصحیح ایرج افشار. تهران،

بنگاهٔ ترجمه و نشر کتاب، ۱۳۴۷.

Estakhri, Abu Eshaq Ebrahim. *Masalek va Mamalek*. A Persian version of a tenth-century Arabic work by an unknown translator of the eleventh or twelfth century.

بیضائی، قاضی ناصر الدین عبدالله بن عمر. *نظام التواریخ*. بتصحیح

بهمن کریمی. تهران، علمی، ۱۳۱۳.

Beiza'i, Qazi Naser al-Din Abdallah b. Amr. *Nezam al-Tavarikh*. Edited by Bahman Karimi. A brief history of Fars, written in the late thirteenth century by the famous scholar and chief judge.

جعفری، جعفر بن محمد بن حسن *تاریخ یزد*. بتصحیح ایرج افشار.

تهران، بنگاه توجمه و نشر کتاب، ۱۳۴۲.

Ja'fari, Ja'far b. Mohammad b. Hasan. *Tarikh-e-Yazd*. Edited by Iraj Afshar. Composed in 845/1441.

حافظ ابرو، شهاب الدین عبدالله بن لطف‌الله بن عبد الرشید خوافی.

ذیل *جامع التواریخ رشیدی*. بتصحیح خان بابا بیانی. تهران،

علمی، ۱۳۱۸.

Hafez Abru [Shehab al-Din Abdallah b. Lotfallah b. Abd al-Rashid Khwafi], *Zeil Jame' al-Tavarikh-e-Rashidi*. Edited by Khan Baba Bayani. This work covers the period from the death of Hulagu Khan to 817/1414. The later, more detailed sections deal with the Timurids. Hafez Abru's work is considered a model of historiography for its clarity, use of sources, and impartiality.

خواندمیر، غیاث الدین. *حبیب السیر*. تهران، خیام، ۱۳۳۳. سه جلد.

Khwandmir, Ghiyath al-Din. *Habib al-Seyr*. Composed in 905/1499.

خورموجی، محمد جعفر الحسینی. *فارسنامه*. محل انتشار نامعلوم.

تالیف در سال ۱۳۷۶ ه. ق.

Khowrmowji, Mohammad Ja'far Al-Hoseini. *Farsnameh*.

رشید الدین، خواجه فضل‌لله طبیب. *تاریخ مبارک غازانی*. بتصحیح

بتصحیح کارل یان. لندن، انتشارات گیب (Gibb)، سری جدید،

شمارهٔ ۱۴. ۱۹۴۰ میلادی.

Rashid al-Din, Khwajeh Fazlallah Tabib. *Tarikh-e-Mobarak-e-Ghazani*. Edited by Carl
Yahn. A work by the noted physician and great minister of the Il-khans.

رشید الدین، خواجه فضل‌لله طبیب. *مکاتبات رشیدی*. بتصحیح محمد

شفیعی. لاهور، انتشارات پنجاب، ۱۹۵۴ میلادی.

Rashid al-Din, Khwajeh Fazlallah Tabib. *Mokatebat-e-Rashidi*. Edited by Mohammad
Shafi'i.

روزبهان، ابو محمد بن ابی نصر البقلی فسائی شیرازی. *عبهر العاشقین*.

بتصحیح محمد معین و بتصحیح و ترجمهٔ هنری کربین. تهران،

انستیتوی ایران و فرانسه، ۱۳۳۷/۱۹۵۰.

Ruzbehan, Abu Mohammad b. Abi Nasr al-Baqli Fasa'i Shirazi. *Abhar al-Asheqin*. Edited
by Mohammad Mo'in and Henri Corbin. A work by Sheikh Ruzbehan Baqli (d. 1210),
the great sufi master of Shiraz.

زرکوب، معین الدین ابو العباس احمد بن ابی الخیر شیرازی. *شیرازنامه*.

بتصحیح اسماعیل واعظ جوادی. تهران، بنیاد فرهنگ ایران، شمارهٔ

۱۲۳. ۱۳۵۰.

Zarkub, Mo'in al-Din Abu al-Abbas Ahmad b. Abi al-Kheir Shirazi. *Shiraznameh*.
Edited by Esma'il Va'ez Javadi. One of the key biographical and geographical sources
of this book. Its exact date of composition is uncertain, with some parts completed in
1343 and others in 1356. It is sketchy in political history, but supplements the *Tarikh-e-
Vassaf* for the Il-Khanid period.

شیرازی، معین الدین جنید بن محمد باغنوی. *شد الازار فی حط الاوزار عن*

زوار المزار. بتصحیح محمد قزوینی و عباس اقبال. تهران، مجلس، ۱۳۲۸.

Shirazi, Mo'in al-Din Joneid b. Mohammad Baghnovi. *Shadd al-Izar fi Hatt al-Wizar
'an Zawar al-Mazar*. Edited by Mohammad Qazvini and Abbas Eqbal. A basic source

for this book. Although essentially a biographical dictionary, this work, composed in 791/1389, contains a wealth of valuable information on the geography, politics, families, and social life of fourteenth-century Shiraz. Qazvini's notes to this work are in themselves masterpieces of scholarship. Ghani, for whatever reason, did not make use of this book in composing his history of the period.

شیرازی، عیسی بن جنید باغنوی. ملتمس الاحبا خالصاً من الریا (هزار مزار).

شیراز، احمدی و جهان نما، ۱۳۲۰.

Shirazi, Isa b. Joneid Baghnovi. *Moltames al-Ahba Khalesan min al-Riya* [*Hezar Mazar*]. A Persian translation of *Shadd al-Izar* by the author's son, usually known by its popular title of *Hezar-Mazar*. A very poor edition.

فرصت شیرازی، میرزا. آثار عجم. بتصحیح عبدالله تهرانی. بمبئی، نادری، ۱۳۴۵

ه‍ . ق.

Forsat Shirazi, Mirza. *Asar-e-Ajam*. Edited by Abdallah Tehrani. A nineteenth-century geography of Fars.

فسائی، حاج میرزا حسن حسینی. فارسنامهٔ ناصری. تهران، سنائی، ۱۳۰۴ ه‍ . ق.

Fasa'i, Haj Mirza Hasan Hoseini. *Farsnameh-ye-Naseri*. A virtual encyclopedia of information about Fars. This work is in two parts: the first, a chronicle of events in Fars from the Islamic conquest to the author's lifetime (in the Qajar period); the second, a description of the physical and social geography of Fars. An invaluable work that would profit by a careful editing.

فصیح خوافی، احمد بن جلال الدین محمد. مجمل فصیحی. بتصحیح محمود

فرخ. مشهد، باستان، ۱۳۳۹. سه جلد.

Fasih Khwafi, Ahamad b. Jalal al-Din Mohammad. *Majmal-e-Fasihi*. Edited by Mahmud Farrokh. A chronicle of events to the year 845/1441. Although emphasizing the history of eastern Iran, this work is valuable for establishing the dates and order of events and for including information not found elsewhere.

قاشانی، ابو القالم عبدالله بن محمد. تاریخ الجایتو. بتصحیح مهین حمبلی.

تهران، بنگاه ترجمه و نشر کتاب، ۱۳۴۸.

Qashani, Abu al-Qalem Abdallah b. Mohammad. *Tarikh-e-Oljaitu*. Edited by Mahin Hambali.

قزوینی، حمدالله مستوفی. نزهت القلوب. بتصحیح محمد دبیر سیاتی.

تهران، طهوری، ۱۳۳۶.

Qazvini, Hamdallah Mostowfi. *Nozhat al-Qolub.* Edited by Mohammad Dabirestani. One of the standard sources for the geography of fourteenth-century Iran.

کاتب، احمد بن حسین بن علی. *تاریخ جدید یزد.* بتصحیح ایرج افشار.

تهران، انتشارات ایران زمین، ۱۳۴۵.

Kateb, Ahmad b. Hosein b. Ali. *Tarikh-e-Jadid-e-Yazd.* Edited by Iraj Afshar. Records events, mostly in Yazd, until 862/1458.

کتبی، محمود. *تاریخ آل مظفر.* بتصحیح ع. ح. نوائی. تهران، ابن سینا، ۱۳۳۴

Kotbi, Mahmud. *Tarikh-e-Al-e-Mozaffar.* Edited by A. H. Nava'i. The author served in the Mozaffarid court, and his concise, unornamented style makes this work a valuable source for the history of the Mozaffarids and Injus.

نطنزی، معین الدین (آنونیم اسکندر). *منتخب التواریخ معینی.* بتصحیح

ژان اوبن. تهران، خیام، ۱۳۳۶.

Natanzi, Mo'in al-Din [the anonymous Eskandar], *Montakhab-e-Tavarikh-e-Mo'ini.* Edited by Jean Aubin. A history of the world from the creation to the death of Timur in 807/1405. Written in 816/1413, this edition includes sections on the history of southern and eastern Iran during the thirteenth and fourteenth centuries.

یزدی، معین الدین علی معلم. *مواهب الهی.* بتصحیح سعید نفیسی. تهران،

اقبال، ۱۳۲۶.

Yazdi, Mo'in al-Din Ali Mo'allem. *Mavaheb-e-Elahi.* Edited by Sa'id Nafisi. Kotbi's *Tarikh-e-Al-e-Mozaffar* is a simplification of this bombastic work, written in 767/1366.

SECONDARY PERSIAN-LANGUAGE SOURCES

اسلامی ندوشن، محمد علی. *ماجرای پایان ناپذیر حافظ.* تهران:
انتشارات یزدان، ۱۳۶۸.

Eslami-ye-Nodushan, Mohammad Ali. *Majara-ye-Payan-na-pazir-e-Hafez.* Tehran: Yazdan Publishing, 1368/1989.

اقبال آشتیانی، عباس. *تاریخ مغول.* تهران، امیر کبیر، چاپ سوم، ۱۳۴۸.

Eqbal Ashtiani, Abbas. *Tarikh-e-Moghul.* A basic secondary work on the history of Iran in the thirteenth and fourteenth centuries. A lack of sourcing detracts from the value of this very learned study.

امداد، حسن. *شیراز در گذشته و حال.* شیران، اتحادیهٔ مطبوعاتی فارس،

۱۳۳۹.

Emdad, Hasan. *Shiraz dar Gozashteh va Hal.*

بهروزی، علی نقی. *بناهای تاریخی و آثار هنری جلگهٔ شیراز.* شیران، ادارهٔ

فرهنگ و هنر، ۱۳۴۹.

Behruzi, Ali Naqi. *Banaha-ye-Tarikhi va Asar-e-Honari-ye-Jolgeh-ye-Shiraz.*

بهروزی، علی نقی. *مسجد جامع شیراز.* شیران، ادارهٔ فرهنگ و هنر، ۱۳۴۹.

Behruz, Ali Naqi. *Masjed-e-Jame'-e-Shiraz.*

بیانی، شیرین. *تاریخ آل جلایر.* تهران، انتشارات دانشگاه، شمارهٔ ۱۰۹۳. ۱۳۴۵.

Bayani, Shirin. *Tarikh-e-Al-e-Jalayer.*

پطوشفسکی، آی. پ. *کشاورزی و مناسبات ارضی در ایران - عهد مغول.*

بترجمهٔ کریم کشاورز. تهران، مؤسسهٔ مطالعات و تحقیقات اجتماعی،

شمارهٔ ۳۴-۳۵. ۱۳۴۴. دو جلد.

Petrushevsky, I. P. *Agriculture and Landholding in Iran—the Mongol Period.* Translated by Karim Keshavarz. A Persian translation of a Russian original. A valuable study of a neglected field. Some of the information in this work is summarized in the author's chapter in volume 5 of the *Cambridge History of Iran: The Seljuk and Mongol Periods.*

دانشپژوه، محمد تقی. *روزبهان نامه.* تهران، انجمان آثار ملی، شمارهٔ ۶۰. ۱۳۴۷.

Daneshpezhou, Mohammad Taqi. *Ruzbehan-nameh.*

دهخدا، علی اکبر. *لغتنامهٔ دهخدا.* تهران : مؤسسهٔ انتشارات و چاپ دانشگاه

تهران، ۱۹۹۴/۱۳۸۳. ۱۴ جلد.

Dehkhoda, Ali Akbar. *Loghatnameh-ye-Dehkhoda.* The great dictionary of the Persian language in fourteenth volumes.

رجائی، احمد علی. *فرهنگ اشعار حافظ.* تهران، زوار، ۱۳۴۰.

Raja'i, Ahmad Ali. *Farhang-e-Ash'ar-e-Hafez.* A valuable and thorough study of the sufi terms in Hafez's poetry.

زرین کوب، عبد الحسین. *از کوچهٔ رندان.* تهران، تهران، انتشارات جیبی، ۱۳۴۹.

Zarin-kub, Abd al-Hosein. *Az Kucheh-ye-Rendan.* A fascinating account of Hafez as he related to the political and social realities of his city. The author's unique combination of scholarship, clear prose, and imagination makes this a most readable and unique source.

سامی، علی. *شیراز ٓ دیار سعدی و حافظ.* شیران، موسوی، چاپ دوم، ۱۳۴۷.

Sami, Ali. *Shiraz: Diyar-e-Sa'di va Hafez.* The author's obvious love of his native town has led him to collect almost everything written by anyone about Shiraz.

ستوده، حسین قلی. *تاریخ آل مظفر.* تهران، انتشارات دانشگاه، گنجینۀ تحقیقات

ایرانی، شمارۀ ۵۱–۵۲. ۱۳۴۶–۴۷. دو جلد.

Setudeh, Hosein Qoli. *Tarikh-e-Al-Mozaffar.* The author's discussion of sources (vol. I, pp. 1–57) is very thorough. Much of the first volume updates Ghani's work.

سجادی، سید جعفر. *فرهنگ لغت و اصطلاحات و تعبیرات عرفانی.* تهران، طهوری،

۱۳۵۰.

Sajadi, Seyyid Ja'far. *Farhang-e-Loghat va Estelahat va Ta'birat-e-Erfani.* A valuable dictionary of sufi terminology.

غنی، قاسم. *بحث در آثار و افکار و احوال حافظ.* جلد اول؛ *تاریخ عصر حافظ.*

تهران، زوار، ۱۳۲۱.

Ghani, Qasem. *Bahs dar Asar va Afkar va Ahval-e-Hafez.* Vol. 1. A leisurely study of the history of Iran in the fourteenth century.

لوی حبیب. *تاریخ یهود ایران.* تهران، بروخیم. ۱۳۳۹. سه جلد.

Levi, Habib. *Tarikh-e- Yahud-e-Iran.*

محلاتی، صدر الدین شیرازی. *دار العلم شیراز.* شیراز، معرفت، ۱۳۴۱.

Mahallati, Sadr al-Din Shirazi, *Dar al-Elm-Shiraz.*

مصطفوی، سید محمد تقی. *اقلیم پارس.* تهران، انتشارات انجمن آثار

ملی، شمارۀ ۴۸. ۱۳۴۸.

Mostafavi, Seyyid Mohammad Taqi. *Eqlim-e-Pars.* A guide to historical remains in Fars province.

مهران، رحمت‌الله. *بزرگان شیراز.* تهران، انتشارات انجمن آثار ملی، شمارهٔ

۶۴. ۱۳۴۸.

Mehraz, Rahmatallah. *Bozorgan-e-Shiraz.*

ندیمی، غلام حسین. *روزبهان یا شطاح فارس.* شیران، احمدی، ۱۳۴۵.

Nadimi, Gholam Hosein. *Ruzbehan, ya Shattâh-e-Fars.*

واجد شیرازی، محمد جعفر. "شرح سه بیت بزبان شیرازی از روزبهان"

راهنمای کتاب، سال سیزدهم، شمارهٔ ۱۱-۱۲ (دی-اسفند ۱۳۴۹).

Vajad-e-Shirazi, Mohammad Ja'far. "Shahr-e-Seh Beit be Zaban-e-Shirazi az Ruzbe-han." From *Rahmena-ye-Ketab.*

PERSIAN POETRY

حافظ، خواجه شمس الدین محمد شیرازی. *دیوان.* بتصحیح انجوی شیرازی

تهران، جاویدان علمی، ۱۳۴۵.

Hafez, Khwajeh Shams al-Din Mohammad Shirazi. *Divan.* Edited by Enjavi Shirazi. Includes a useful introduction on the social, political, and cultural conditions of Hafez's time.

زاکانی، مولانا نظام الدین عبید. *کلیات.* بتصحیح عباس اقبال. تهران، اقبال،

۱۳۴۶.

Zakani, Mowlana Nezam al-Din Obeid. *Kolliyat.* Edited by Abbas Eqbal.

Zakani, Mowlana Nezam al-Din Obeid. *Cats against Rats.* Translated by Mas'ud Farzad. London: The Prioy Press, 1945.

شیرازی، معین الدین جنید بن محمد باغنوی. *دیوان.* بتصحیح سعید نفیسی،

تهران، مرکزی، ۱۳۲۰.

Shirazi, Mo'in al-Din Joneid b. Mahmud Baghnovi. *Divan.* Poetry by the author of the fourteenth-century *Shadd al-Izar.*

شیرازی مولانا بسحق حلاج، مشهور به شیخ اطعمه. *دیوان.* شیران، معرفت.

تاریخ انتشار نامعلوم.

Shirazi, Mowlana Boshaq Hallaj, [known as *Sheikh At'ameh*]. *Divan.* The famous fourteenth-to-fifteenth-century "poet of food" whose verses are full of reworked mystical imagery.

PRIMARY SOURCES IN ENGLISH TRANSLATION

Gibb, H. R. et al., editors and translators. *The Travels of Ibn Battuta.* Cambridge: University Press for the Hakluyt Society, 1962. Three volumes.

LeStrange, G., translator. *Clavijo's Embassy to Tamerlane, 1403–06.* The Broadway Travellers. London: Routledge and Sons, 1928.

———. *Nuzhat al-Qulub of Hamdu'llah Mustawfi [Mostowfi] Qazvini.* Gibb Memorial, vol. 23, no. 2. London, 1919.

Minorsky, V., editor and translator. *Hudud al-Alam.* Gibb Memorial, new series, vol. 11. London, 1937.

OTHER SECONDARY SOURCES

Arberry, Arthur J. *Classical Persian Literature.* London: George Allen and Unwin, 1958.

———. *Fifty Poems of Hafiz.* Cambridge: University Press, 1962.

———. *Shiraz: Persian City of Saints and Poets.* Norman: University of Oklahoma Press, 1960.

Bausani, Alessandro. *The Persians.* Translated from the Italian by J. B. Donne. London: Elek, 1971.

Bill, James Alban. *Politics of Iran: Groups, Classes, and Modernization.* Columbus, Ohio: Charles E. Merrill, 1972.

Bosworth, Clifford Edmund. *The Ghaznavids.* Edinburgh: University Press, 1963.

———. *The (New) Islamic Dynasties.* New York: Columbia University Press, 1996.

Boyle, J. A., editor. *The Saljuq and Mongol Periods.* Vol. 5 of *The Cambridge History of Iran.* Cambridge: University Press, 1968.

Browne, Edward G. *The Tartar Dominion (1265–1502).* Vol. 3 of *A Literary History of Persia.* Cambridge: University Press, 1920.

———. *A Year Amongst the Persians.* London: Adam and Charles Black, 1950.

Bulliet, Richard W. *The Patricians of Nishapur.* Harvard Middle Eastern Studies, no. 16. Cambridge: Harvard University Press, 1972.

———. "The Shaikh al-Islam and the Evolution of Islamic Society." *Studia Islamica* 35 (1972): 53–67.

Clarke, John I. *The Iranian City of Shiraz.* Department of Geography Research Papers, no. 7. Durham, England: 1963.

Ernst, Carl W. *Ruzbihan Baqli: Mysticism and the Rhetoric of Sainthood in Persian Sufism.* Richmond England: Curzon Press, 1996.

Fisher, W. B., editor. *The Land of Iran.* Vol. 1 of *The Cambridge History of Iran.* Cambridge: University Press, 1968.

Frye, Richard N. *Bukhara: The Medieval Achievement.* Norman: University of Oklahoma Press, 1965.

Frye, Richard N., editor. *Sassanian Remains from Qasr-i Abu Nasr.* Cambridge: Harvard University Press, 1973.

Gray, Basil. "Iranian Painting of the Fourteenth Century." *The Iran Society* 1, no. 5
(January 17, 1938): 50–58.

————. *Persian Painting.* Geneva: Skira World Publishing, 1961.

Hourani, A. H. and S. M. Sterne, editors. *The Islamic City.* Oxford: Bruno Cassirer,
1970.

Lambton, A. K. S. *Landlord and Peasant in Persia.* London: Oxford University Press,
1953.

Manz, Beatrice Forbes. *The Rise and Fall of Tamerlane.* Cambridge: Cambridge University Press, 1993.

Melikian-Chirvani, Asadullah Souren. "Le Royaume de Salomon." *Le Monde Iranien
et l'Islam* 1 (n.d.): 1–41.

Perry, John R. "Toward a Theory of Iranian Urban Moieties: The *Haydariyyah* and
the *Ni'matiyyah* Revisited." *Iranian Studies* 32, no. 1 (Winter 1999): 51–70.

Potter, Lawrence G. "Sufis and Sultans in Post-Mongol Iran." Iranian Studies 27, nos.
1-4 (1994): 77–102.

————. *The Kart Dynasty of Heart: Religion and Politics in Medieval Iran.* Unpublished
thesis. Columbia University, 1992.

Russell, C. J. "Late Ancient and Medieval Population" *Transactions of the American Philo-
sophical Society,* new series, vol. 48, no. 3 (1958).

Rypka, Jan et. al. *History of Iranian Literature.* Dordrecht, Holland: D. Reidel, 1967.

Whitcomb, Donald S. *Before the Roses and Nightingales. Excavations at Qasr-i Abu Nasr,
Old Shiraz.* New York: Metropolitan Museum of Art, 1985.

Zaryab, Abbas. "The Struggles of Religious Sects in the Court of the Ilkhanids and
the Fate of Shi'ism in that Time." *Iran Shinasi* 2, no. 2 (Summer 1971): 103–106.

INDEX

Pages with illustrations are indicated in boldface type; tables are indicated in italic type.